# Legendary
# Yachts

# Legendary Yachts

TEXT &
PHOTOGRAPHY BY:

Gilles Martin-Raget

DRAWINGS BY:

François Chevalier

INTRODUCTION BY:

Matthew P. Murphy

Abbeville Press Publishers

New York  Paris  London

# Contents

| | |
|---|---|
| Introduction | 7 |
| *Avel* | 8 |
| *Pen Duick* | 16 |
| *Shenandoah* | 26 |
| *Moonbeam III* | 34 |
| Rendezvous: Porto Cervo | 42 |
| *Tuiga* | 48 |
| *Orion* | 56 |
| *Mariette* | 64 |
| *8-m class* | 72 |
| Rendezvous: Monaco Classic Week | 82 |
| *Kentra* | 88 |
| *Creole* | 96 |
| *Dorade* | 104 |
| *Lelantina* | 112 |
| Rendezvous: Royal Cannes Regattas | 120 |
| *J-class* | 128 |
| *Altair* | 138 |
| *Oiseau de feu* | 148 |
| Rendezvous: Brest-Douarnenez | 156 |
| *Thendara* | 162 |
| *12-m class* | 170 |
| *Agneta* | 180 |
| Rendezvous: The Nioulargue | 188 |
| Glossary | 198 |

# Introduction

Nothing stirs the imagination quite the way beautiful classic yachts do. Organic, even alive, these vessels are distillations of natural forces, highly skilled craftsmanship, and cool-headed sailing talent. They are time machines: when a fleet of vintage yachts moves past bucolic landscapes unblotted by modern sights, it transports us back a hundred or more years.

Vintage yachts appeal to all of the senses. They are a visual treat, to be sure, but they are also a delight to the ears as they part tons of ocean water at their bows, while whispered commands catalyze ballets of on-deck activity. They thrill the nose and taste buds with mingled scents of varnish, pine tar, seawater, and wood. They stimulate the hands, inviting caresses that mimic the actions that brought them to life: the plane strokes of carpenters, the flourishes of painters, the deft, nimble fingers of riggers.

Nothing else like classic yachts calls upon such a rare set of skills — flawless joinerwork and finishing, traditional rigging, and competent sailing. Indeed, some of the individuals who restore or maintain these boats derive their satisfaction only from these creative activities. Others find the sailing to be their source of pleasure. And still others find the simple act of watching all of this happen to be their delight. The yacht is a symphony of labor, skill, love, and years.

Each one of the vessels in the following pages has a powerful story — a colorful birth, often a protracted period of neglect, and, finally, an unlikely rebirth accomplished by owners and craftspeople of single-minded, steadfast determination. The yachts are time capsules, but their histories are more than simple lists of money spent and races won. They reflect values spanning the entire twentieth century, from launchings during an era when skilled craftsmanship was so much a part of everyday life, through wartime idleness, to postwar futurism, when much of the world turned its back on skilled handwork. Many of the boats featured herein spent inauspicious years on dry land or mud banks, or in services far beneath their true potential. This book celebrates the most recent trend: a renaissance of traditional boatbuilding skill, rigging, sailmaking, stewardship, and simple appreciation.

The renaissance itself has elevated a handful of men and woman to visionary status in the world of vintage yachts. The team at Fairlie Restorations in England appears repeatedly in this book, for it is perhaps without peer in the sheer tonnage and quality of fine yachts saved. And likewise, the name of rigger Harry Spencer has become synonymous with the perfectionism and attention to detail required in the fitting out of these craft. And among the owners, there's perhaps none so well known as the American Elizabeth Meyer, whose restoration of the J-class yacht *Endeavour* is one of the most ambitious ever undertaken.

The culmination of this renaissance has been the establishment of races and rallies for large classic vessels held all over Europe. Among even the most casual sailors, the names of these events evoke images of forests of masts and white-uniformed crews working in silent coordination. The most celebrated of the gatherings — Porto Cervo, Monaco Classic Week, Brest–Douarnenez, Royal Cannes Regattas and the most well known, the Nioulargue — form the backbone of this book, for it was at these that the author and photographer Gilles Martin-Raget has encountered many of these fine craft firsthand.

The sailing of these yachts at rallies requires a delicate blend of competitiveness and restraint, for the vessels are actually irreplaceable works of functional art — but functioning is the *sine qua non* of their existence. A boat that is used is, generally, a happy boat, while a boat that spends her days at the dock tends to suffer a spiral of deterioration that increases exponentially over the years. There are no wallflowers in the collection presented here; all of the boats are icons in the world of classic yachting.

Each boat's story is unique, and some of these tales have heartbreaking twists — like the tragic loss of Éric Tabarly from his beloved William Fife-designed cutter *Pen Duick*. Others are as unlikely as they are magnificent, such as the restoration of the ketch *Kentra*.

In the following pages, Martin-Raget captures the essence of these tales in words and images, while François Chevalier provides beautiful drawings of each boat. The effect, like the boats themselves, is much more than the sum of its parts.

Matthew P. Murphy
Editor, *WoodenBoat* Magazine

## AVEL
## The marvelous toy

1896

Avel was born a very long time ago, in 1896, in the south of England. This makes her one of the oldest traditional yachts that can still be seen sailing today. Originally, this little gaff-rigged cutter was the brainchild of one of the most famous naval architects of the modern era: Charles E. Nicholson. At the beginning of the twentieth century, he was responsible for the basic design of several hundred boats — each as fast as it was elegant. For all his Englishness, he was really a European before his time, which was a true mark of originality in an age when the motto "Britannia rules the waves" was everywhere in evidence. Growing up under the tutelage of a father who already owned a well-known shipyard for pleasure yachts, he was able to attract new clients from abroad, particularly from France. That is how Avel came to be built, because it was ordered not by a British yachtsman but by a well-off resident of the French port of Nantes — a man of independent means called René Calame, who in his time owned a large number of yachts.

Avel, which means "wind" in the Breton language, was conceived as a cruiser. She was the second boat of this name to be ordered by René Calame from the yard of Camper & Nicholson, and later there was even a third. Built in only four months at Gosport, near Portsmouth in southern England, and launched on May 14, 1896, she was a relatively classical yacht for her time apart from two remarkable characteristics: a concave stem (the reverse of most classic yachts) and a keel line parallel to the waterline. These were no doubt designed to help her cope with the hazards of navigating at low tide. She was showered with praise by the nautical press of the day, and remained only a short time in the hands of her first owner. After two years she was sold to a British enthusiast, who kept her for only a few months before letting her go to a third owner in 1899. Things were more stable for Avel over the next fifteen years, but she then passed through a dozen different owners until she was finally dropped from the British shipping register on January 11, 1927. That was the end of the first chapter.

OPPOSITE
Avel *sailing with the wind on the beam toward the Rock of Monaco with all her sails out. She is remarkable for the refined nature of her rigging, but it takes a good dozen arms to maneuver this boat, which today is the oldest operational sailing vessel in the world.*

## AVEL

Architect: C. E. Nicholson
Yard: Camper & Nicholson
Launched: 1896
Restored: 1994
Overall length: 18.25 m (59 ft 10 in)
Waterline length: 12.58 m (41 ft 3 in)
Maximum beam: 3.50 m (11 ft 6 in)
Draft: 2.30 m (7 ft 7 in)
Displacement: 26.6 t
Sail area: 183 sq m (219 sq yd)

ABOVE AND LEFT
*Builder's name engraved on the rudder head; detail of the bow decorated in gold leaf; yacht's compass. Avel, like all her fellow yachts, is scrupulously maintained — the eye for detail extends as far as the dress of the crew.*

The second part of Avel's life lasted sixty-five years and was not exactly glorious. In her favor, she had at least kept her old ribs in good condition. Already out of service for several years, she then began a new career as a houseboat on the mudbanks off West Mersea to the northeast of London. As the years passed, her keel and rigging were placed into service aboard some other yacht and a cabin was added to the deck along with various other fittings needed for her role as a dwelling. So there she was, stuck fast in a domestic existence that was of little value except that it protected her from the indignities to which racing boats were often subjected, and also from the stormy weather which has seen off many such boats on the mudbanks of Britain. So much for her second chapter of life.

Enter William Collier, a British expert in classic yachts; John Bardon, a British skipper of classic yachts; and Maurizio Gucci, an Italian owner of classic yachts, and scion of the Gucci empire. These three men, familiar figures in the world of traditional yachts, now turned their efforts, each in his own way, to the task of reviving Avel.

Driven by his research into old yachts, and particularly those built by Camper & Nicholson, the journalist and historian William Collier made several visits to the West Mersea area. He must have noticed this hull with the stem that made it so unusual. Then, after delving more closely into its origins, he discovered its fine pedigree and visited its owner several times. So when he was approached by John Bardon, skipper of Creole, who was looking for a small boat to restore on behalf of Maurizio Gucci, William Collier saw it as his dreamed-of chance to get Avel out of the mud — which is what they did.

The next part of the story features an exemplary restoration under the leadership of a rigger named Harry Spencer. The boat was transported to his yard in Cowes on the Isle of Wight, off the south coast of England, and there they worked on her between 1993 and 1994. Spencer carried out the long and exacting project in collaboration with Clark Posten, an American marine carpenter from the Mystic Seaport museum in Connecticut, and D. Lami, a specialist recruited in Spain who was responsible for rebuilding the deck. The boat turned out to be in a considerable shambles. They had to demolish the deck, which was beyond repair, before carefully removing the interior fittings, which proved to be in excellent condition. They had to replace the stem, 60 percent of the ribs and the whole of the iron frame, and

remake the framework of the stern. They also had to replace the deck and the superstructure completely and — most difficult of all — redesign and reconstruct all the rigging, since neither the original rigging nor the plans for it were to be found. The latter were in fact discovered once the work had been finished, and they revealed that Avel was now carrying more sail and less ballast than before.

Among her characteristics today, her gracious silhouette is impossible to miss in any gathering of traditional yachts: she is always the boat that heels and pitches the most! Her extremely long bowsprit serves only to magnify the ceaseless rocking which her hull goes into as soon as the seas are any size at all. On the other hand, the slightest little breeze allows her to get underway faster than her competitors, and the elegant gaff-rigged cutter, which may sometimes seem like a plaything in the midst of the much larger boats around her, sails much more easily in a light wind than most of her mates.

ABOVE RIGHT
Avel sailing close-hauled in mild conditions.

PAGES 12–13
Avel taking part in a regatta at Cannes. The crew has rigged a boom to break out the big white spinnaker. In such conditions, the main task for the helmsman is to keep the boat moving.

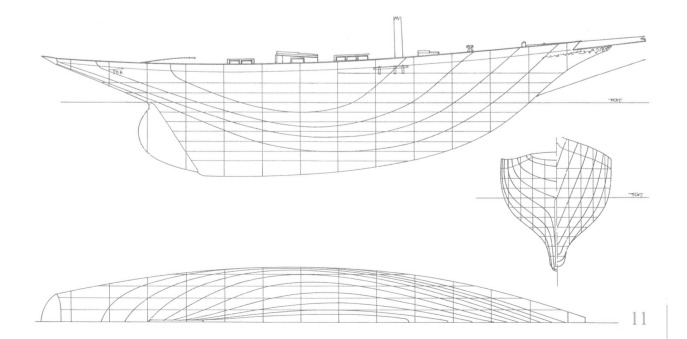

It hardly needs stating that *Avel* is remarkably well maintained — it could not be otherwise. More than that, ever since she was relaunched, her owner has made sure that the turnout of the crew matches the reputation of the Gucci label, and the slightest detail, from the fastening of a scarf to the angle of a cap or the way the cuffs of their unbleached linen pants are rolled up, is continually under scrutiny. *Avel* is always to be seen in the company of the big schooner *Creole*, to which she is sometimes moored, like a chick watched over by its mother hen. There is just one slight difference, however: these two boats belong to a very exclusive club — that of the world's most beautiful sailing yachts!

ABOVE
*The crew at work in a rising sea ...*

LEFT
*Hauling on the staysail in a good breeze. A crewman leans all his weight on the sheet while another secures the line round a cleat. On board Avel all maneuvers are made by hand without a winch.*

## PEN DUICK
### A hundred years of passion

"Dad, you can't do that!" The despairs of youth can mark a whole life — especially when there is no alternative but to act like a brat in front of the man who has come to buy the family boat. He must be shown, and with punctilious zeal, every fault, every potential problem, every source of trouble on the boat — "It's a really old boat, isn't it?" — until this horrible person finally turns on his heel and gives up. The battering he receives from his father afterwards will also be memorable, but at least he has achieved his goal: *Pen Duick*, the Tabarly family's boat, will not have been sold on that particular day.

Éric Tabarly's passion for his boat is an abundant source of anecdotes from more than fifty years of life together — fifty years of a passionate love which was sometimes sidelined during long periods of separation, but which always returned for whole seasons of trouble-free sailing. Gradually this passion took on its own exclusive and defining rhythm — the rhythm of the cruise, which nothing could ever alter. It was *Pen Duick*, the fine old family boat in which his love for sailing had first been awakened, that Éric kept for his old age, and was the one he used for all his pleasure cruises.

*Pen Duick* was born a very long time ago, well before Guy Tabarly, Éric's father, committed himself to acquiring her in 1938. In fact, this little gaff-rigged cutter was called *Yum* when she emerged in 1898 from the drawing board of William Fife III. She was an elegant little racing boat, but it cannot be denied that she was by no means as beautiful as she is today.

She had been commissioned by a Mr. Cummins, an Irishman living in Cork, and built in a local yard. She took part in several regattas beginning the year after she was launched. As the seasons went by, she passed through the hands of some fifteen different owners, some of whom sailed only on cruises and others only in regattas. Her name was changed several times as she became, in succession, *Grisélidis* (in 1902, the year she arrived in France), *Magda* (1908), *Grisélidis* again (1910), *Cora V* (1919), *Astarté* (1924), *Panurge* (1931), and *Butterfly* (1933) before she was finally christened *Pen Duick* — which means "coal tit" in Breton — by her 1935 owner, Jean Lebec. It was the Lebec family, well known at La Trinité-sur-Mer in Brittany, who sold *Pen Duick* to Guy Tabarly in a deal that would secure the entry of this already legendary name in the history of sailing and ocean racing.

OPPOSITE
*Éric Tabarly's boat* Pen Duick, *close-hauled under reduced sail, dives into the waves during a regatta in the Mediterranean.*

ABOVE
*Éric Tabarly, here shown remaking a splice, lavished attention on* Pen Duick. *Their time together will endure as the perfect example of one man's total passion for his boat.*

Éric was only a child when he sailed on her for the first time. It was on this physically and technically demanding boat that he discovered his love for sailing. Here on this deck he learned the joys of maneuvering a boat, and here at this helm he became a skipper for the first time, took charge in his first races, made his first starts, learned to tack well and forged his passion for racing on the open sea. With *Pen Duick*, too, Éric Tabarly developed his formidable skill for using the most innovative techniques to create boats that were ahead of their time.

It was in 1952 that Éric became the fifteenth owner of *Pen Duick*. The boat was feeling her age and needed to be worked on, and Éric's father, refusing to take on the job, chose instead to give the boat to his eldest son. This was also the time when Éric enlisted and became a pilot in the Naval Air Service, leaving for Saigon and there living a monastic existence, saving up every franc from his salary to be able to restore his boat. On his return, he faced some very bad news: *Pen Duick* was too worn out, her very structure had eroded, and she was only good for the breakers' yard.

Although dismayed, he could not bring himself to get rid of her. Moved by the same enthusiasm which had driven him a few years earlier to scupper his father's attempts to sell the boat, he dreamed up an impossible idea: to use the old hull as a mold and clad it all round with a hull made of glass fiber and resin. At that time, no one had made such a big boat in plastic. The work, carried out at La Trinité-sur-Mer with the help of the Costantini yard, took three years and swallowed up all Éric's savings as well as his leave time. He removed the deck and the whole of the interior, took out the ballast, turned the hull over, prepared it, hired workers to cut the seven layers of glass fiber, laid them on with resin,

sanded them down, coated them, sanded them down again, used timber spars to turn the hull over on a day when there was a high tide, and replaced the ballast.

The yard was then asked to destroy the original hull, which was still stuck inside the new plastic one. Then they had to remake all the wooden parts, make a new deck and install the basic interior fittings. While this was going on, Éric redesigned and made up a larger rigging, and threw out the old cotton sails. The long-awaited day at last arrived, *Pen Duick* took to the sea again — and promptly lost her mast on her first outing! This disaster was quickly remedied with the help of an anonymous donor, and the boat, then the largest ever to be made of polyester resin, was at last able to sail.

Now we have reached the time when the unknown Breton officer, gnawed by his passion for ocean racing, began to sail craft which grew ever bigger, ever faster, and ever crazier — and became the famous Éric Tabarly. He won races, toured the world, sailed every ocean, and became a celebrity. All this time *Pen Duick* had to resign herself to waiting — for twenty-one years …

The day finally came when, having come almost full-circle, Éric slowly began to form an idea which had lain buried in the deepest recesses of his mind — the idea that *Pen Duick* would one day sail again. He took the plunge in

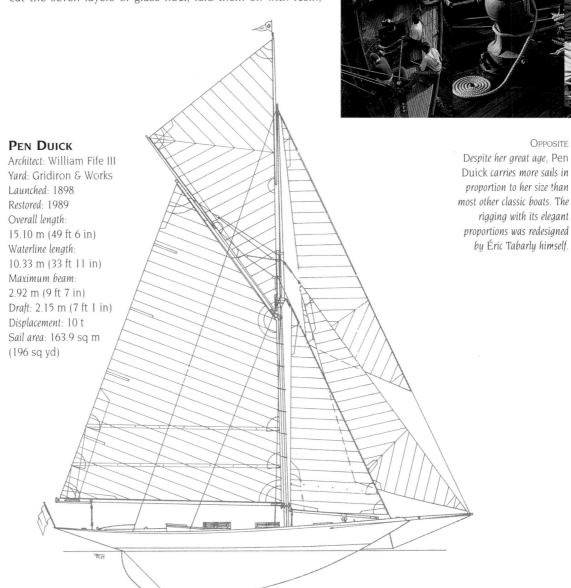

**PEN DUICK**

Architect: William Fife III
Yard: Gridiron & Works
Launched: 1898
Restored: 1989
Overall length:
15.10 m (49 ft 6 in)
Waterline length:
10.33 m (33 ft 11 in)
Maximum beam:
2.92 m (9 ft 7 in)
Draft: 2.15 m (7 ft 1 in)
Displacement: 10 t
Sail area: 163.9 sq m
(196 sq yd)

OPPOSITE
*Despite her great age, Pen Duick carries more sails in proportion to her size than most other classic boats. The rigging with its elegant proportions was redesigned by Éric Tabarly himself.*

ABOVE
*You need muscle power at the helm of Pen Duick. The center picture shows the capstan, used for weighing anchor.*

1983, entrusting Raymond Labbé with the task of restoring the boat at his yard in Saint-Malo. To escort her there from Le Crouesty, he employed an original method which only he could have imagined: he used his new sailing craft Pen Duick IV to tow Pen Duick under sail. The enterprise almost ended in disaster as they approached Saint-Malo, when a blast of wind caught them off the Île de Batz.

The third rebirth of Pen Duick was to take six years to fulfill, during which time Raymond Labbé's team of carpenters could only work slowly, in tune with Éric's finances. They concentrated on the fittings, which they remade in the old style using mahogany complete with moldings, and on installing a small motor. Things went faster later on, thanks to a grant from the city of Rouen, which wanted Pen Duick to take part in a great regatta scheduled for July 9, 1989. The completed work was superb: Pen Duick had once again become a magnificent classic small yacht that was more beautiful than ever thanks to the splendid proportions of her new, more slender rigging.

From then on, Pen Duick sailed off to a happy future. Fife's old boat took up racing once more, tacking away on cruises, parading her majestic silhouette at all the finest regattas, such as at Brest or on the Mediterranean circuit, sailing alongside the most prestigious yachts in history, and heading off on cruises appropriate to her prestige to places like Scotland and the Azores. It was fun to be pampered by one of the greatest sailors of all time, and to spend peaceful hours moored at Bénodet in western Brittany. She seemed to smile to herself when Éric brought along his daughter Marie to sail on the craft she called "the boat that sails on a slant."

And then there was the magnificent occasion of her hundredth birthday. For the first time, a regatta was

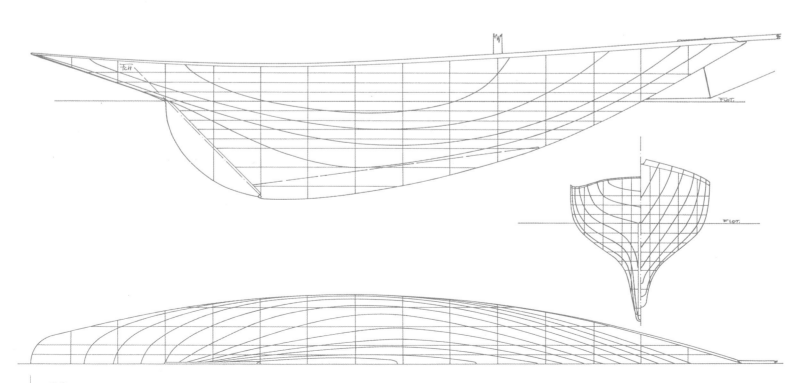

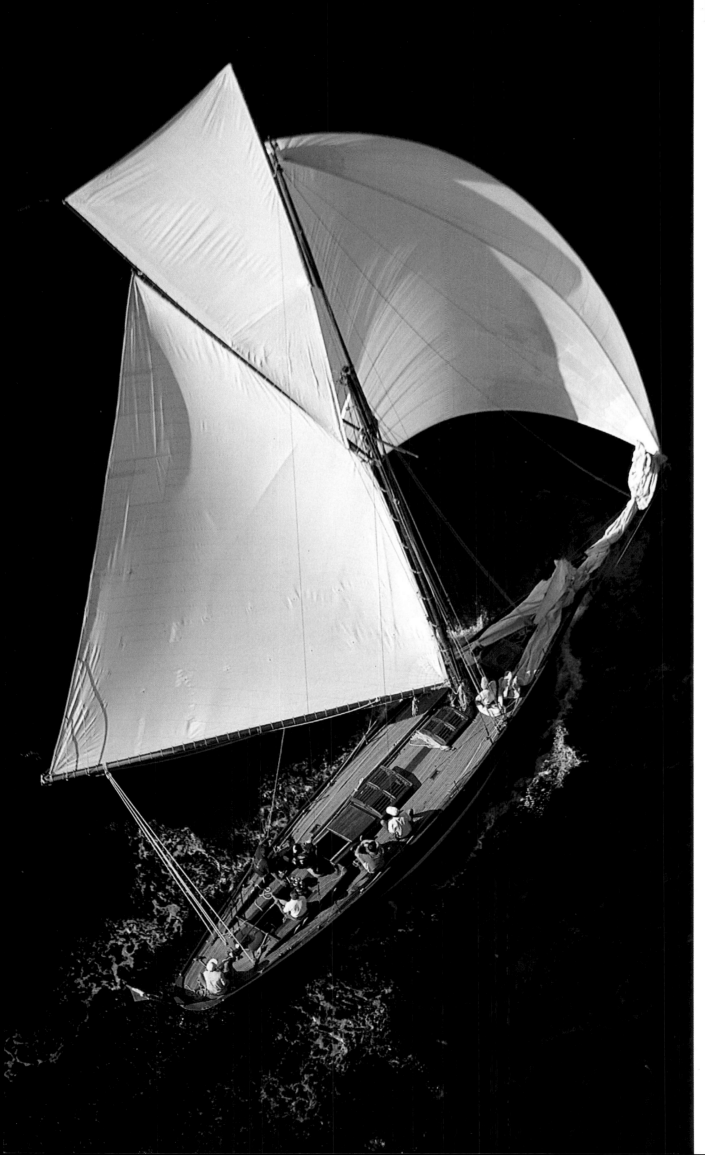

LEFT
*Running before the
wind,* Pen Duick *flies
a large asymmetrical
spinnaker rigged to
the end of the
bowsprit, which
removes the need
for a boom.*

organized to celebrate the centenary of a boat, and *Pen Duick* was the queen of the party. Her descendants *Pen Duick* II and *Pen Duick* IV came too. Some of the most venerable classic yachts, such as *Tuiga*, *Moonbeam*, and *Kentra*, had also made the trip up from their far-off Mediterranean homes to Bénodet to pay homage to her splendid rigging, endowed for the occasion with a new set of sails. The sea swarmed with boats, there was a party on shore, and much laughter and singing. Éric Tabarly was blissfully happy and looked twenty years younger. He was even more overjoyed to think that he and his boat would be sailing off in the next few days to southwest Scotland. They would be cruising up to Fairlie, where there was to be a regatta for boats designed by Fife. By a strange stroke of fate, this return to her roots, this pilgrimage to the birthplace of *Pen Duick*, was to be the sailor's last voyage. In total darkness in the middle of the Irish Sea, sailing from Cork to Fairlie, *Pen Duick* killed the man who had restored her to life. She was rolling badly, causing her to club him brutally and send him flying into the sea to join the vanished sailors of legend. It was a clean break, frankly executed, without tears or reunions. For the thousands of people who loved him as a man and admired him as a sailor, it was a sudden, dramatic, and immense loss. There was great sadness and emotion, and incomprehension too — for *Pen Duick* had sailed on toward Scotland to go and weep in the arms of her sisters. Do love affairs ever end?

ABOVE
*Éric Tabarly preparing his boat in May 1998, on the eve of the centenary celebrations for* Pen Duick. *A few days later he was to die at sea while sailing in flotilla toward Fairlie. The great family of* Pen Duick *boats, indeed the entire maritime world, would be orphaned by his loss.*

# SHENANDOAH
## The model schooner

Few yachts have had such a turbulent, full, or prestigious life as *Shenandoah*. Confounding every fashionable notion, she is one of the most beautiful sailing ships that can still be seen sailing today.

*Shenandoah* is, and always has been, a high society boat. The man who brought her into the world was a very wealthy North American banker and member of the New York Yacht Club, Gibson Fahnestock. People in his family lent money to governments, founded banks and worked at the stock exchange. He it was who asked the American architect Theodore Ernest Ferris, a man who specialized in big vessels, notably cargo and steamships, to design him "a solid boat, with a good steel hull, fast and comfortable, and with enough room to stock provisions for several weeks and quarters for a sizeable crew," so that he could spend his old age aboard her in the Mediterranean. Gibson Fahnestock was 50 years old when the boat was launched in 1902 by the Townsend & Downey yard at Shooter Island on Newark Bay, New Jersey. She returned to Newport, Rhode Island, and two years later undertook the crossing to Europe. The voyage lasted two weeks as she was frequently becalmed and sailing ships at that time were clearly not equipped with an engine.

Her next owner was a German, which brought about her first name change — from *Shenandoah* to *Lasca II* — and led to her becoming a prisoner of war, as she was in England in 1914. In 1919 she was bought by Sir John Esplen and fitted with a motor, and then sold on to another British yachtsman, Godfrey Williams, before passing under the Italian flag and changing her name to *Atlantide*. Her new owner, Prince Ludovico Potenziani, gave her the luster which goes so well with her silhouette, but he could not resist an offer from a very well-heeled Dane named Viggo Jarl, who in 1929 not only bought the boat but took on her Italian crew. Viggo Jarl may not have been a prince but he mixed with great world figures: the Duke and Duchess of Windsor stayed on board, as did King Umberto of Italy, King Baudouin of Belgium and his father Léopold, and the sovereigns of Denmark. As far as his boat was concerned, Viggo Jarl was a true king. He carried out a thorough maintenance program, had the motors changed again, and installed a generator. Based in Cannes, the boat did a lot of sailing before and after World War II (18,000 miles

**OPPOSITE**
*Completely restored in New Zealand in 1996, Shenandoah recovered all the grace of her original rigging. She is one of the greatest classic boats presently sailing.*

**ABOVE**
*The figurehead on the prow represents Shenandoah, a Native-American chief described in a traditional American song.*

ABOVE
*The principal saloon,*
*like rest of the boat,*
*is decorated in a style*
*which creates a perfect*
*match between*
*maritime tradition*
*and the owner's taste*
*for oriental culture.*

a year) until she was sold once more in 1952. After the era of the princes, *Atlantide*, as she was still called, entered a more uncertain period involving offshore society, Genovese brokers, the Caribbean, even contraband, and which ended decisively when she was sequestrated by the French state. She was to endure ten years of inactivity and deterioration before she could recover all her former glory.

The man who brought her back to life was named Marcel Bich. He was a passionate follower of the America's Cup and regularly sailed out of Newport in his twelve-meter yachts. Following a serious bout of restoration, *Shenandoah* recovered her name and, soon after, her original sailing patch on the open seas off the coast of New England. She became the flagship of a lord and master whose poor performance at sea was accompanied by a flamboyance ashore which staggered the world. *Shenandoah* served as a floating host, receiving guests and giving lavish receptions, and adapted to it all very well. Her masts were shortened and flanked by an enormous deckhouse, but she performed her worldly role with flair. She remained under the ownership of the Bich family until 1986, when she found herself in the new role of charter vessel; then she changed owners again and took on a few Swiss characteristics. She made several appearances at the

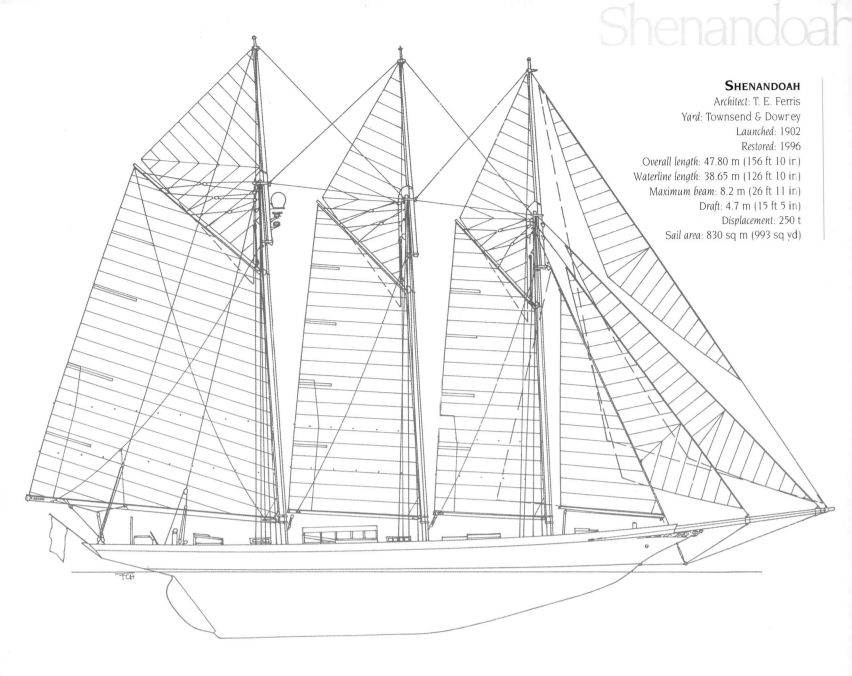

**SHENANDOAH**
*Architect:* T. E. Ferris
*Yard:* Townsend & Downey
*Launched:* 1902
*Restored:* 1996
*Overall length:* 47.80 m (156 ft 10 in)
*Waterline length:* 38.65 m (126 ft 10 in)
*Maximum beam:* 8.2 m (26 ft 11 in)
*Draft:* 4.7 m (15 ft 5 in)
*Displacement:* 250 t
*Sail area:* 830 sq m (993 sq yd)

Nioulargue under an Asian crew, then went to the Far East for further commercial endeavors.

But *Shenandoah* wanted more. Most of all there were serious repairs that had to be done. Faithful restorations were then in vogue, and a new European owner plunged into the massive task of fully restoring her prestige and her original appearance at the same time. It needed more than courage to start again from scratch. It is never pleasant to uncover nasty surprises when you are restoring a ten-meter boat, but at least the solutions are on a human scale. When you are dealing with a large yacht of the size and age of *Shenandoah*, the problems rapidly become enormous. The work was carried out in New Zealand at the yard of McMullen & Wings, with the help of the architect Martin Francis and under the supervision of a new skipper named Serge Guilhaumou. It was to take all of two-and-a-half years.

When *Shenandoah* returned to Europe, at the close of the 1997 season, she had never looked so beautiful. Apart from the globe covering the telephone antenna, she had recovered her true original appearance. With the deckhouse gone, her hull only seemed longer. Enormously lightened, the boat rediscovered all her speed under sail and could make way with the help of the slightest breeze.

RIGHT
*Crew's eye view from aloft in the rigging.*

PAGES 30–31
Shenandoah *going at full speed during a windy regatta off* Antibes.

Modern equipment had been fitted too, of course, but so discreetly that it was barely noticeable either on or below deck. Apart from the mizzen, the sails were always hoisted by hand, and the winches which worked the halyards were all large capstans fitted with pawls, which demanded good teamwork from the crew.

When she took part in a regatta, *Shenandoah* consumed the crew's energy at a furious rate. It took forty-five minutes to raise all the sails, and in a moderate breeze they had to collapse and reset the three jibs on every tack. The interior arrangements had been completely remade and were superb, in a decorative style that combined tradition with the owner's taste for Asian culture.

Today *Shenandoah* is taken on testing voyages. She is to make a long trip out to Auckland, via the Magellan Strait, to celebrate the America's Cup 2000.

*OPPOSITE*
*To steer Shenandoah in the midst of other classic yachts requires dexterity, prudence and good powers of anticipation. The sails have to be checked constantly.*

*BELOW*
*The crew, who may number up to thirty in a race, always includes a few tightrope walkers who can if necessary work in the rigging. Taking down the great spinnaker requires all hands to be present on deck.*

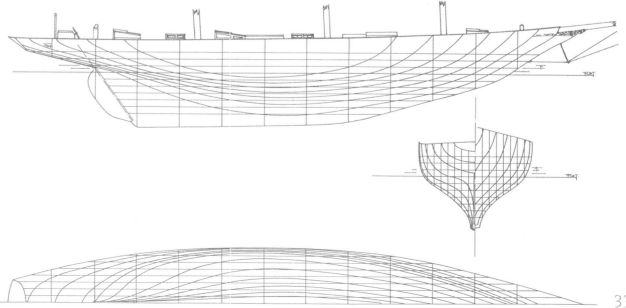

# Moonbeam III
## The Scottish lord

**M**oonbeam is inevitably compared with *Tuiga*. The two boats date from the beginning of the twentieth century, have similar origins, their silhouettes are much alike, and they are the same size. Even today, the two gaff-rigged cutters meet at classic regattas, challenge one another, sail round the same buoys, and, back at the quayside, are moored in the same area. Both were designed by William Fife III and built in the family yard at Fairlie. Everything points to their being similar, but in essence they are very different boats.

Where *Tuiga* displays a slenderness verging on the delicate, *Moonbeam* offers something more rugged, more authentic, more maritime. Is it her rigging — less extreme than it once was? Is it that higher stem, so characteristic of Fife's designs, which gives her a slightly rougher, more aggressive look? Is it the more elevated freeboard which makes her seem a little stouter? *Moonbeam* seems more solid, better suited to facing rough weather and high seas. *Tuiga* has something female, and Latin, about her. *Moonbeam* is masculine, Anglo-Saxon, even Celtic.

Launched in 1903, six years before *Tuiga*, *Moonbeam* was built when the rules governing racing were different from those affecting her favorite opponent. While *Tuiga* was clearly conceived as a fifteen-meter boat, conforming to the international specifications drawn up in 1906, *Moonbeam* was designed a few years earlier under the rules of the Royal Ocean Racing Club, which had been revised in 1900. This made her broader in the beam, heavier by about twenty tons, carrying more ballast and with a current sail area that is slightly less than that of *Tuiga*, even though their individual shapes are similar. Because of these factors she is more at ease in windy conditions, whereas *Tuiga* prefers lighter breezes.

ABOVE
*Blocks and tackle and a chest, lined up at the foot of the mast.*

OPPOSITE
*Moonbeam (sail no. 88) in a regatta off Monaco with Tuiga (sail no. D3). It is a sight yachting people never tire of witnessing. Aside from their sail numbers, the two boats, though very similar to look at, have stems which are discernibly different.*

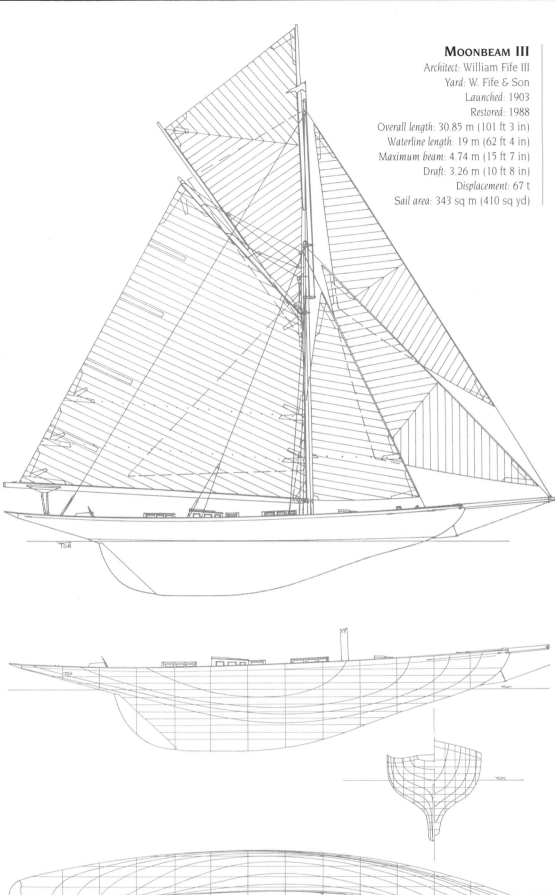

# MOONBEAM III

*Architect:* William Fife III
*Yard:* W. Fife & Son
*Launched:* 1903
*Restored:* 1988
*Overall length:* 30.85 m (101 ft 3 in)
*Waterline length:* 19 m (62 ft 4 in)
*Maximum beam:* 4.74 m (15 ft 7 in)
*Draft:* 3.26 m (10 ft 8 in)
*Displacement:* 67 t
*Sail area:* 343 sq m (410 sq yd)

Aside from their general appearance, the one thing that binds *Moonbeam* and *Tuiga* forever is the signature of the architect who designed them both.

Try to imagine what the name Fife meant right at the beginning of the twentieth century: it was a real institution, a mark of the highest quality in matters of boat construction; the firm's designs for racer–cruisers were a guarantee of their speed. Sometimes people even came from America, which in those days was no small undertaking, to order a Fife design, and this at a time when the New World was already swearing its allegiance to the talents of Nathanael Herreshoff, the wizard of Bristol, Rhode Island. Unfortunately, little is known of the three William Fifes who made such a mark in the nineteenth century with their numerous designs for beautiful boats, and nothing remains of the original yard at Fairlie. In 1905, about a year before the launch of *Moonbeam III* (the 491st boat bearing the Fife signature), Lloyd's of London registered an astonishing total of 326 boats constructed around the Clyde estuary between Glasgow and the sea. Today, many of these boats are still sailing, their owners proudly displaying the maker's emblem: a Chinese dragon, its mouth open, placed at the end of the colored border strip which runs the length of the hull.

The London lawyer Charles Plumtree Johnson, a member of the Royal Yacht Squadron and the Royal Thames Yacht Club, was a regular customer at the yard, having already bought the two previous *Moonbeams* from Fife. The first, acquired in 1858, was the concept of William Fife II. *Moonbeam II*, a 42-ton cutter "built by Fife of Fairlie," replaced her in 1899. She was not entirely satisfactory in terms of speed, and so a few years later her owner ordered a new boat: *Moonbeam III*.

OPPOSITE,
TOP TO BOTTOM
*Detail of the cockpit;
the central saloon;
detail of a small side
desk; a guest cabin;
close-up of a cleat
made of teak and
bronze, its ends well
worn through use.*

PAGES 38–9
*Perched on the end of
the bowsprit,
a crewman tries to
raise the great
asymmetrical
spinnaker even though
the wind is too light.*

*Moonbeam III* was originally rigged as a yawl with two masts — the mizzen, known as the jigger, being visibly shorter than the mainmast. Only later was she converted into a gaff-rigged cutter.

ABOVE
*The emblem of boats
built by Fife adorns
the stern of
Moonbeam; detail
of the mast-hoops of
the mainsail piled
together; another clash
between Moonbeam
and Tuiga.*

In 1920, *Moonbeam III* crossed the English Channel to Brest, her new home port. She had been sold to a Monsieur Maroni, an industrialist from Paris. We pick up her traces again in 1948, now in the Mediterranean, where she became the property of Félix Amiot, an aviation pioneer and founder of Constructions Mécaniques de Normandie. Curiously, he was to leave her on dry land for twenty-three years. Later *Moonbeam III* became a charter vessel under her new owner, Madame Anthony, before she was bought by Dr. John Poncia, who had her shipped back to England in 1979 to undergo a major restoration at the yard of Camper & Nicholson in Shamrock Quay, Southampton. The work, supervised by John Sharp, was not completed until 1988.

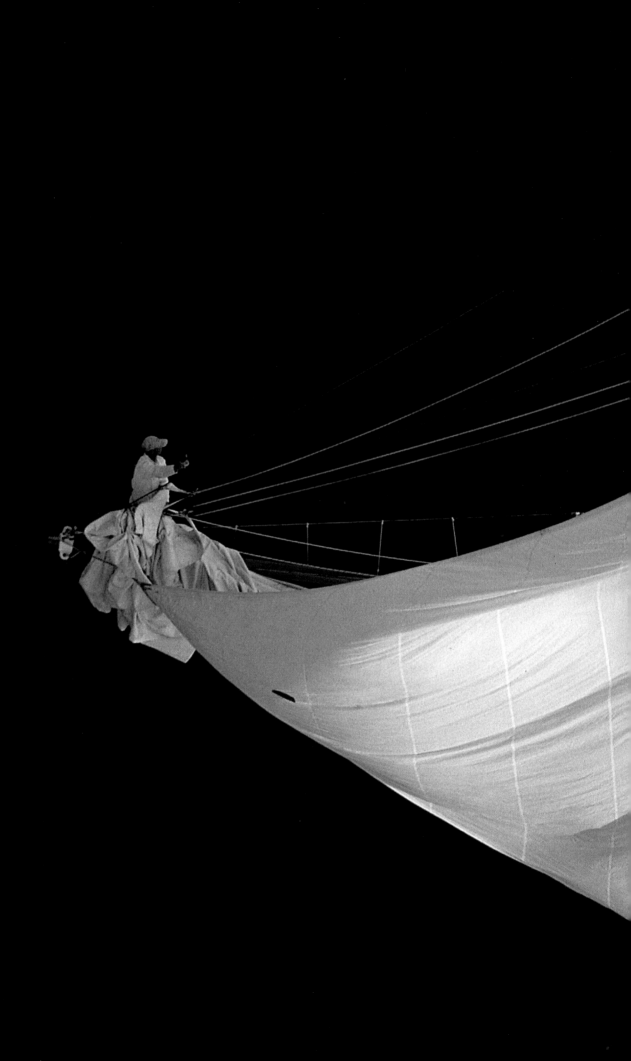

RIGHT
*Beneath the gaze of
ideally situated
spectators,
Moonbeam
rounds the turret of
La Moutte during a
regatta at the
Nioulargue.*

The restoration of *Moonbeam* was a little less extreme than that of *Tuiga*. The deck was equipped with several winches — a modification justified by the different displacements of the two boats. *Moonbeam* is a much tougher boat and much more physical. She was fitted with a steering wheel, whereas her rival was allowed to retain her tiller. Subsequently, *Moonbeam* has had two owners, who took her to Cannes, where she is presently in the hands of Philippe Lechevallier, one of France's best skippers of classic yachts. As is certain of her fellow boats, she eats up a lot of money on maintenance and has essentially become a charter vessel. She sails from prestigious events to regattas of traditional yachts, taking part in so many that sometimes her old limbs creak a little. Once she lost her mast and in 1997 she was unable to compete in a duel with *Tuiga* for the Dole Trophy, arranged for the height of the Cannes Festival. Never mind: in June 1998 *Moonbeam* bravely completed two voyages around the Iberian Peninsula, heading for Bénodet in Brittany to celebrate the centenary of *Pen Duick*, and then off to Fairlie for a family reunion with other boats designed or built by one the three Fifes. But then, yachts are surely made to be sailed!

BELOW
*Standing at the helm of a boat like* Moonbeam *in a steady wind is an intensely pleasurable experience. You have the unmatchable feeling of sailing an authentic witness to the history of yachting.*

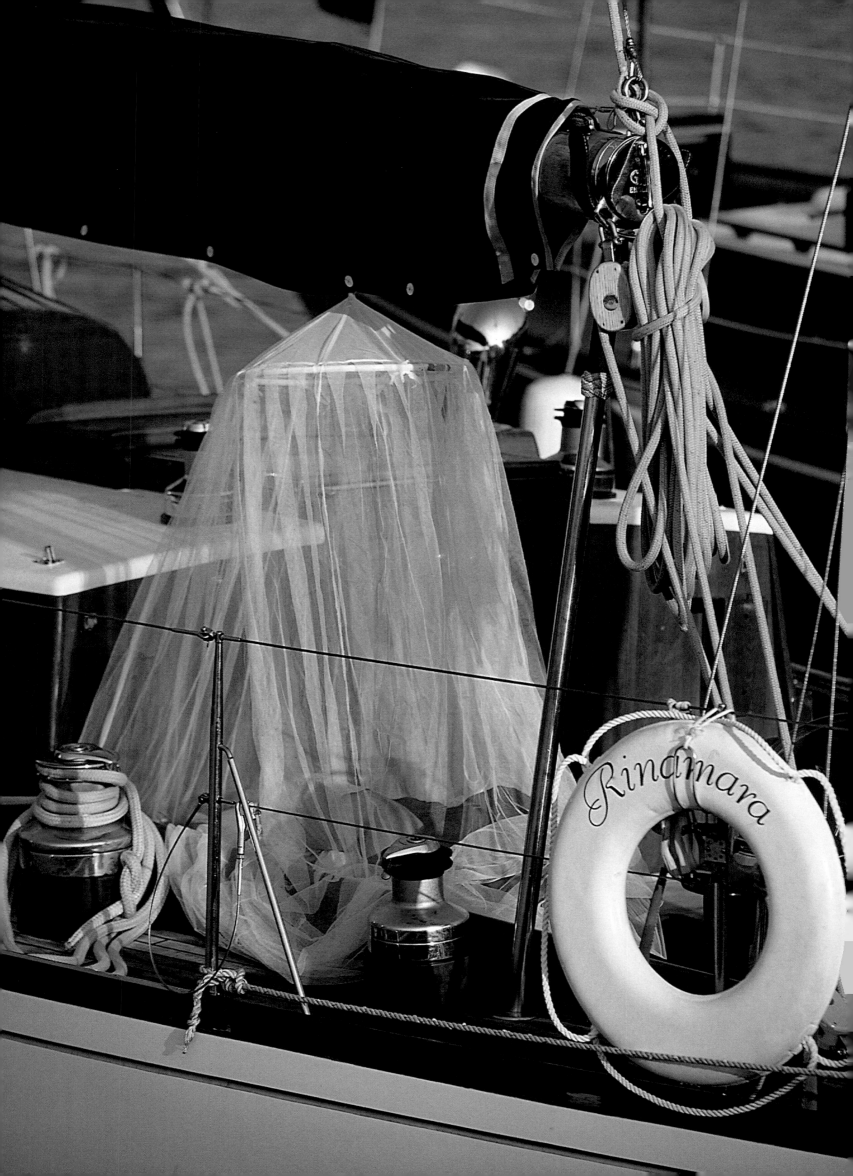

# Porto Cervo

**Lying in the north-east of Sardinia, protected from the open sea by the Maddalena Archipelago, the Costa Smeralda (Emerald Coast) has in twenty years become one of the essential calling places for the most beautiful yachts on this planet.**

Under the aegis of the Aga Khan, who developed a luxury apartment complex around Porto Cervo that is remarkable both for the quality of its architecture and the way it integrates with the countryside, yachting has been associated from the beginning with the development of this site, and has seen it rapidly grow in prestige. Rallies for international yachts in contention for the America's Cup, the Sardinia Cup (which brings together the finest racing prototypes), and the Semaine des Bouches (a gathering of amateur racing cruisers), have raised the Costa Smeralda to the ranks of the world's most famous rendezvous locales, on a par with Cowes, Newport, or Saint-Tropez. The Sardinian venue was very quick to launch its regatta for traditional yachts, at a time when this was not yet fashionable, and when classic yachts were far fewer in number and in poorer condition than they are today. From then on, what has become the San Pellegrino Trophy event takes place every odd-numbered year, in the first week in September — a time when the living is particularly good in that part of the Mediterranean.

### How it all came about

It was natural for Italy to be the host nation for this kind of gathering, as the majority of classic yachts currently under sail fly the transalpine flag. It was also quite understandable that the first meetings should have taken place in Sardinia, which is a natural cruising destination for all boats based in Italy, given that a number of owners have a pied-à-terre on the

Costa Smeralda. And we should not forget that the nearby island of Maddalena is a well-established center for restoring lateen-rigged boats. The largest island in the archipelago has a number of attractive-looking yards specializing in the construction of traditional craft. Every two years, a few miles to the west at Stintino, there is a tremendous reunion of those marvelous lateen-rigged boats that you can see all along the Mediterranean coasts of Spain, France, and Italy.

Finally, Porto Cervo is a place where boat owners always find it a pleasure to visit, whether they have the good fortune to own a modern racing boat or a classic yacht. The Maddalena Archipelago sets the standard for fine moorings, embellished with turquoise seas and crystal waters. Corsica is not far away across the Straits of Bonifacio, neither is the Lavezzi Archipelago. The wind, on average, is a little more consistent than

elsewhere in the Mediterranean, and the regatta course, which you can pick out amongst the maze of islands and islets of the Maddalena Archipelago, seems to stretch forever.

## Where the living is good

One the special features of Porto Cervo's "veteran boat rally" is the way the classic yachts have to maneuver and almost scrape their way past the great pale granite rocks at the very heart of the archipelago. The waters are sheltered, the wind is playful, and the light is constantly changing. You can normally sail in a thermal breeze which has the good taste not to exceed force four, and if by chance the mistral should blow more than is reasonable, the boats stay in harbor and the crews, their daily tasks of polishing and shining the brass completed, need no persuading to take advantage of the innumerable white sandy beaches around Liscia di Vacca.

*ABOVE*
*Large yachts, narrow alleys, and colorful rocks are all part of the Sardinian atmosphere.*

*OPPOSITE*
*The lighthouse on the Monaci Islands is one of the favorite racing marks of the Costa Smeralda Yacht Club. But don't cut it too close …*

*PAGES 46–7*
*The flotilla of classic yachts moored beneath the village, where you can hear the crickets sing, smell the maquis as it transmits its perfumed odors, and discover some enchanting bays nearby. Porto Cervo at the end of summer is never disagreeable — on the contrary, it is a rendezvous that should on no account be missed …*

At the event, which every other year opens the Mediterranean classic yacht season, the boats gather beneath the old village, where many an agreeable evening is spent in the little square, the air filled with the scent of the maquis. The races are planned to allow for several days' rest during the week, leaving time to go sailing along the Cala de Volpe close to the beautiful Gulf of Sardinia, whose appearance could make you think you were closer to Ireland — an unlikely thought, however, given the dryness of the atmosphere around these parts. Another pleasant tradition is for participants in the San Pellegrino Trophy to put in, for one evening, at the island of Maddalena. Here the Italian

Marines have a large base close to the NATO establishment, where they are heavily involved in restoring a number of classic yachts for use as training vessels. After the prestigious prize-giving ceremony, made by the Costa Smeralda Yacht Club, whose Prix d'Élégance is certainly the most coveted title, the boats cast off without delay and head north, racing or sailing in convoy back to the European continent to take part in the remaining events of the classic yacht circuit: Monaco, Cannes, and the Nioulargue.

# TUIGA
## A princess
## among yachts

Tuiga is a real marvel — a pure gem, perfection in sailing, harmony in the guise of a yacht. It is impossible to remain unmoved when *Tuiga* sails by — impossible not to be immediately seduced by her perfect silhouette, her total elegance, the ease with which she sails in all conditions. One would search in vain for the slightest fault in her lines, her appearance, her upkeep or in any one of the details which have made her restoration a model of its kind. *Tuiga* has once more become a true work of art — but what a history she has!

When she came into being, in 1909, this Fife design was a pioneer: she was one of the first "fifteen-meter" yachts, one of the new class of racing yachts created after 1906 by the first international yachting conference. There they proposed a return to the past. Since the initial development of yachting, in the middle of the nineteenth century, each country, each region almost, had devised its own way of measuring and racing its boats. At the beginning of the twentieth century, it was virtually impossible for a yachtsman to take part in a regatta overseas, or to organize international regattas, as the boats and the technical rules were never compatible. This was certainly tiresome for foreigners visiting Cowes on the Isle of Wight — the then unchallenged center of the yachting world. So the authorities decided to consult with architects, to carry out studies, and set up a single international ruling body. The meeting to do this took place in London in 1906 and was of great importance for the evolution of all yachting. Among the nine new classes created on this occasion, effective from January 1, 1907, the "fifteen-meter" class quickly caught the attention of the most prominent owners as it corresponded to a size worthy of their status. The two first boats in the series were English, but the king of Spain, Alphonse XIII, a great yacht lover and an indispensable presence at the summer meetings of yachtsmen at Cowes, was very quick to order one of these new boats, which were at the same time both massive and elegant. His was built in Spain to Fife plans and was christened *Hispania*.

RIGHT
*The silhouette of*
Tuiga, *like that of all gaff-rigged cutters, blends supreme elegance with effectiveness under sail.*

OPPOSITE
*A model of fine restoration and faithfulness to the spirit of her original version,* Tuiga's *deck is obviously not equipped with a single winch. Bringing her to requires the efforts of the whole crew to draw the immense mainsail inboard by hand to the center of the boat. In windy conditions, this is an exhausting operation.*

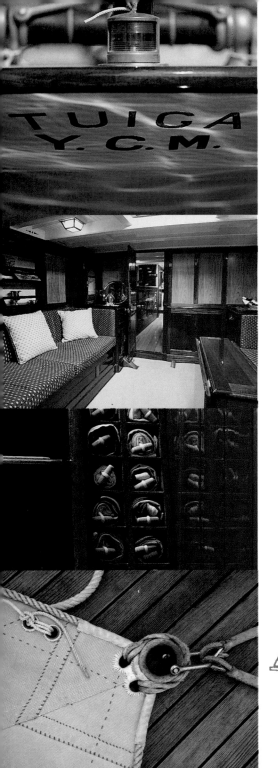

**TUIGA**
Architect: William Fife III
Yard: W. Fife & Son
Launched: 1909
Restored: 1993
Overall length: 28 m (91 ft 10 in)
Waterline length: 14.90 m (48 ft 11 in)
Maximum beam: 4.30 m (14 ft 1 in)
Draft: 3 m (9 ft 10 in)
Displacement: 39 t
Sail area: 370 sq m (443 sq yd)

ABOVE
Every detail, from the door hinges to the compass housing to the finishing work on the sails, was recreated as closely as possible to the original version.

RIGHT
Launched as a response to Hispania, then owned by Alphonse XIII, king of Spain, Tuiga has become the flagship of the Monaco Yacht Club, which demands a total respect for etiquette, especially in the use of flags.

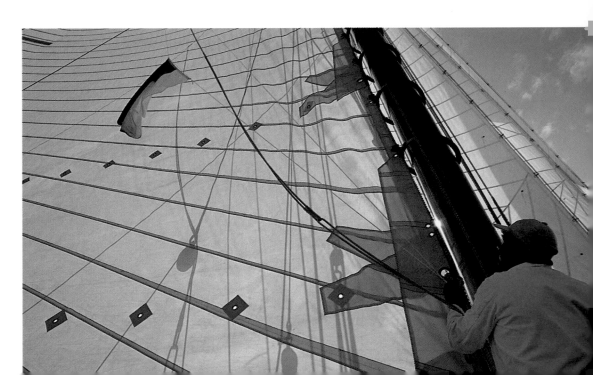

Almost at the same time, one of his intimates, the duke of Medinacelli, also ordered plans from Scottish architect William Fife III for one of these new regatta machines. This was *Tuiga*, built at Fairlie in Scotland in the Fife family yard and launched in the spring of 1909. Without delay, *Tuiga* was tossed into the heat of regatta sailing, and took part in numerous events in Spain, France, England, Scotland, and Ireland. She had a number of victories, leading to a racing career which lasted until World War I. When war broke out, *Tuiga* was obliged to join the migration which saw many yachts of her day going up to Sweden or Norway to be sold so as to escape being requisitioned, which generally meant they disappeared. Lead from the keels of boats was a particularly sought-after material in those troubled times.

Sold in Sweden in 1916, *Tuiga* changed owners several times, was renamed *Betty* IV, returned to England in 1923 to become *Dorina*, and again changed her livery in 1934. Her silhouette evolved considerably at that time. From then on she was given a more efficient Bermuda rig and a short boom which did not clear the transom. She also lost her bowsprit, was fitted with a steering wheel and changed her name to *Krismet* III. In this modified state she took part in her last race before World War II: the Fastnet race of 1935. She was acquired by J. B. Douglas and stayed in that family until 1970, at which time she was renamed *Nevada*, received the rig of the twelve-meter class *Sceptre*, was sent to Piraeus in Greece and used for chartering, but without receiving the maintenance she needed. She was then bought by a French couple who discovered her prestigious origins but lacked the means to give her back her illustrious past. Finally, she went to Cyprus in 1989 as the property of the Swiss collector Albert Obrist, who was already embarked on restoring another marvelous yacht: the Fife-designed *Altaïr*.

*Tuiga*'s second life began disastrously with an escorted voyage to England, during the course of which the boat almost sank for good. The restoration which followed was on a considerable scale, but everything was done to make it exemplary. The task was entrusted to Fairlie Restoration in England, on the banks of the River Hamble near Southampton. Already well attuned after their work on *A'taïr*, the Duncan Walker team accomplished a remarkable task. They dismantled her piece by piece in order to reinforce the metal structure which served as the boat's skeleton, replacing

her planking and rebuilding the deck, which they now covered in yellow pine, as it had been originally, in place of the teak it had acquired. The interior no longer looked anything like it had when the boat was launched, and since the yard did not have the original plans it was rebuilt according to the standards of that era, using other Fife plans which had been better conserved. Apart from a motor and a screw, *Tuiga* recovered all her former looks and luster, including new rigging on the lines of the original, made by Harry Spencer in Colombian pine. As in the days when she crossed the Solent from Cowes, the boat's deck plan was gloriously free of winches. This had been a real challenge for the team members in charge of the boat's sailing qualities, for *Tuiga* displaced nearly 40 tons and had a sail area of 370 square meters (443 sq yd).

In the 1993 season, *Tuiga* was able to join the rallies of classic yachts, and her appearance did not go unnoticed. It was a real shock, not only for all lovers of traditional yachts but also for the other regatta participants present, and for the public in general. Not only was her silhouette a complete delight, but the way her crew sailed her, with a sureness verging on perfection, was a testament to the absolute rightness of her restoration.

ABOVE RIGHT
Detail of the leather
protective covers on the
mast-hoops of the mainsail.
The riggers in the crew have
to change these regularly,
which means a lot of
repetitive work.

PAGES 52–3
Like all fifteen-meter yachts
and, in general, all boats
conforming to international
classes, Tuiga carries a lot
of sail, has a low freeboard
and is somewhat prone
to heeling. Such is the price
of elegance …

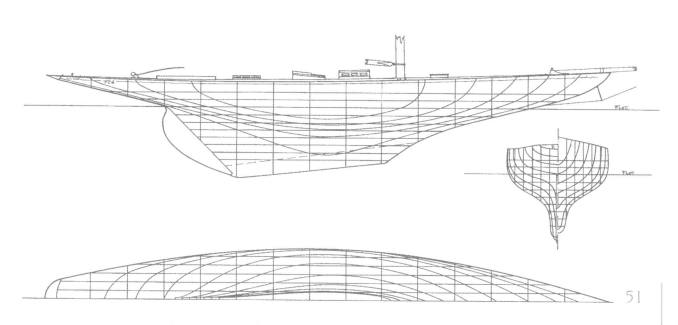

RIGHT
Sailing and maintaining a
yacht such as Tuiga
requires not only an expert
knowledge of old yachts but
also a certain amount of
physical labor. The topsail,
fixed to two wooden spars,
has to be hoisted up from
the foot of the mainmast.

Today *Tuiga* has again changed owners and sails under the colors of the Monaco Yacht Club, whose flagship she has become. The president of the Yacht Club, Prince Albert of Monaco, often sails aboard her and invites top sailors such as Paul Cayard or the architect Doug Peterson to help him. Éric Tabarly loved steering this prestigious and demanding sailing boat for the technical challenge it gave him. You cannot steer *Tuiga* as you would a vessel of carbonfiber. Now once more a princess among yachts, *Tuiga* has lost none of her old elegance and sails between the pick of the rallies and exhibitions as she did in her racing years, and

continues to win at numerous regattas. At the Monaco Classic Week in 1997, she was visited by Juan Carlos, king of Spain, who went down to the saloon with Albert of Monaco just as his ancestor Alphonse XIII used to do. Invited by his host to add some words to the visitors' book, the king drew his inspiration from the great tradition of yachting.

The hull of *Hispania*, *Tuiga*'s old regatta companion, had been rediscovered and was in the process of being restored. In two sentences, Juan Carlos issued a challenge to *Tuiga* to meet her old rival in a regatta, to be organized when *Hispania* was once more ready to sail. History renews itself once more …

ABOVE
*The foremost yachtsmen are regularly invited to sail Tuiga. Éric Tabarly himself loved taking the helm of this boat, which will always be a model of classic beauty. Sometimes it is drenching physical work, but she is so beautiful under sail.*

# Orion
## The pioneering legend

*O*rion belongs to a pioneering race. She is one of the great yachts which, with *Puritan*, *Shenandoah*, and *Altaïr*, one day dared to tie up side by side at Porto Cervo, Imperia, or Saint-Tropez, heralding the rebirth of interest in traditional yachts. Such majesty, such sparkling beauty, such regal magnificence concentrated in such a tiny spot, compelled those who love sailing, as well as people who love exceptional objects, to examine the tremendous heritage embodied in these old yachts.

*Orion* was also one of those boats which dared, despite their great age and fragility, their complex rigging and refined interiors, to line up once more in regattas. Of course, those first races were only a pretext to sail a common course, to make a few tacks together and to unfurl the secrets of sails which most of the time were kept stowed away. At that time, certain captains, better versed in the arts of polishing brasswork than in the rules of the road, were asking over the radio, just minutes before the starting gun, in which direction they should be sailing! So, to start with, the old yachts took part in races mostly for the greater pleasure of their owners and crews. It was a sort of show, a parade, a majestic procession which allowed people to examine the beauty of their rigging, to notice how easily one or the other sailed into the wind or plowed through the waves. At this level, *Orion* was an empress among boats.

People always remember that superb autumn afternoon at Saint-Tropez in 1987. An easterly wind in the Gulf of Genoa had raised a majestic swell, which gave off an iridescent light at the end of the day. The wind had slackened, and *Orion* was strutting about like a senator, with all her sails let out, at the close of an absolutely wonderful race with *Puritan*. Her sails, magnificently displayed, were of an immaculate white. Her bow wave frothed every time a new swell arrived to help her on to the finishing line. *Puritan*, far off in the distance, made a perfect counterpoint.

OPPOSITE
Orion *in a regatta leads* Altaïr *and* Creole, *the latter having already unleashed her immense white spinnaker. Racing aboard great traditional yachts, a delicate and sophisticated exercise in mild weather, is transformed into a veritable commando operation when the wind gets up.*

## ORION

Architect: C. E. Nicholson
Yard: Camper & Nicholson
Launched: 1910
Restored: 1979
Overall length: 44.74 m (146 ft 9 in)
Waterline length: 27.45 m (90 ft 1 in)
Maximum beam: 7.15 m (23 ft 5 in)
Draft: 4.20 m (13 ft 9 in)
Displacement: 254 t
Sail area: 986 sq m (1,179 sq yd)

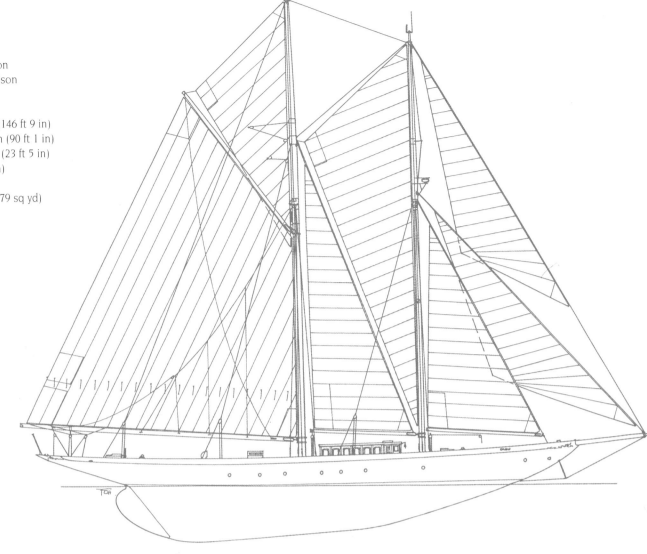

RIGHT
*Every detail is in its place on board Orion: the sailing gear ranged along her bulwarks and at the foot of the mast; inside the doghouse, where the crew can shelter in bad weather; and in the large main saloon, which is equipped with a real fireplace.*

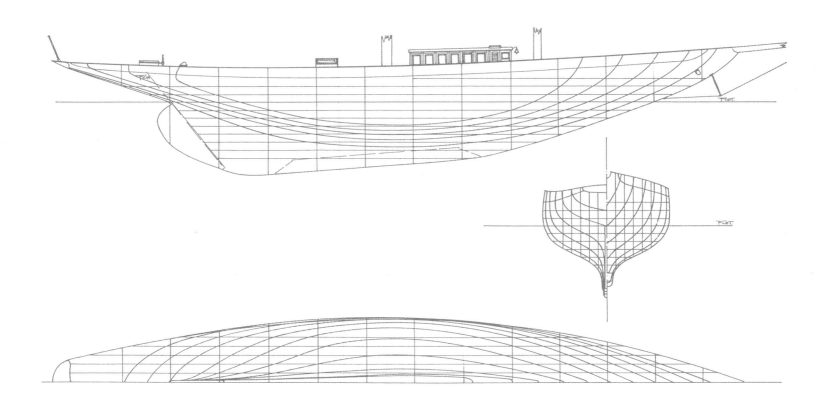

That was still before the time when dozens of small motor boats and sailing dinghies accompanied each of the most beautiful traditional boats. Here was total purity — an absolutely magnificent vision of sailing that could excite the most profound of emotions. The captain decided to pass within a hundred feet or so of the sea wall of that harbor in Provence, where every façade had caught something of the reddish light of evening. It was in magic moments like this that the enthusiasm for traditional sailing boats was reborn. In this capacity, *Orion* was an inspired actor, more so than other boats.

In 1978, *Orion* was one of the first great classic yachts to be so magnificently restored, at a time when this was neither fashionable nor even discussed. It happened simply because she had become the property of a family who felt it their duty to maintain her as one maintains a château, to ensure that this valuable piece of our heritage was not devalued. They saw her as a major work that must be brought to life. She was at once a work of art and a piece of history as well as a yacht capable of taking her hosts on quite exceptional vacations.

Almost 45 meters (147 feet) in overall length, *Orion* is a very big boat — indeed, one of the biggest of all the traditional yachts. Although she has remained an ardent follower of races, she is also one of the heaviest, and the hardest to maneuver under sail over a classic race circuit. She gives a phenomenal impression of power, while her schooner rig gives her a silhouette which lacks nothing in grace or finesse.

ABOVE
*Orion under reduced sail takes the wind from the mountains of the Estérel.*

PAGES 60–61
*Bringing down the mizzen at the end of a regatta in the beautiful light of sunset. It is scenes such as this which have inspired the revival of classic yachts, Orion being one of the pioneers of the movement.*

RIGHT
*A breeze is blowing
but Orion is under
full sail. Here she
toughs it out in
a regatta off
Saint-Tropez.*

Born in 1910 from plans drawn by Charles E. Nicholson, *Orion* is no longer in the prime of youth. In her we can see what the great English schooners looked like at the beginning of the twentieth century, in the golden age of yachting. She was built at Gosport, near Portsmouth in southern England, at the yard of Camper & Nicholson. Legend has it that she was first ordered by the Spanish Royal Family. In reality she was finally delivered, under the name of *Sylvana*, to Lieut.-Col. Morgan, a member of the Royal Yacht Squadron and an eminent British yachtsman.

In 1913 she changed flags and crossed the English Channel to France, having been bought by Count Jean de Polignac, himself a member of the Yacht Club de France. One world war and a few years later, she again changed hands but her new owner, Bunau Varilla, only kept her for two seasons. Still under the French flag, she took the fine name of *Fays de France* in 1921, her fourth owner also being the proprietor of the newspaper *Le Matin*. She returned to England in 1922, where she was rechristened *Diana* by Capt. Cecil P. Slade. In 1927 she was under the colors of Argentina, now renamed *Vira* by her Argentinean owner, Raoul C. Monsegur. She had a spell in Spain from 1930, when Miguel de Pinillos became her owner and gave her her present name, *Orion*. Cherished by further successive owners, she was moored in various harbors, suffered considerable damage from a fire in Le Havre but continued sailing under the Spanish flag until 1967.

Now *Orion* was getting on in years and not receiving the painstaking care she had enjoyed in her youth. Her interior walls were whitewashed, she lost her mast on a convoy between Spain and Marseilles, and was simply abandoned a few months later. In 1978, she was a wreck when she was taken over at La Spezia by her new owners, two Italian brothers who had made up their minds to bring her back to life. *Orion* was delivered to the Beconcini yard and for two years they grappled with the monumental task of restoring her. Having originally been a gaff-rigged ketch, she was now given a mixed rigging with a gaff-rigged mizzen and Bermuda staysails. The interior recovered all its former luster — from decorative blocks in bronze bearing the arms of the boat to furniture of the day and Persian carpets, not to mention the artistic masterpieces, everything was restored, if not to its original state then at least enough to reflect her magnificent status as a great schooner from the beginning of the twentieth century. An exceptional vessel, *Orion* is also the guarantor of that spirit that gives the word "yacht" a sense of savoir-faire along with a firm dose of good taste.

ABOVE
*At difficult moments you need a cool head to bring back the boat in one piece, and most of all to ensure that no one is injured on board. In rough seas a titanic battle takes place between the boat's prow and the waves.*

# MARIETTE
## The spirit revisited

M*ariette* is the work of a great name in naval architecture: Nathanael Greene Herreshoff. This American architect, often nicknamed the Wizard of Bristol, is one of a small group of British and American architects, along with William Fife III, Charles Nicholson, Alfred Mylne, John Alden, and Olin Stephens, who created the most beautiful classic yachts in history which were at the same time the swiftest boats of their time. Nat Herreshoff notably designed seven defenders of the America's Cup between 1893 and 1920, five of them winners. Following the example of Fife, Herreshoff was not only one of the most brilliant naval architects of his day but also a constructor of genius who built his own creations in his yard at Bristol, Rhode Island, where at certain periods over a thousand people were working.

Nathanael Herreshoff was well known for his practice of sculpting a wooden model of the boat he was creating before he made any designs. His first successful boat, *Shadow*, was conceived in 1871, when he was only twenty-two years old and finishing his studies at the Massachusetts Institute of Technology. For a time he worked as an engineer at the Corliss Company which manufactured steam engines, acquiring the technical and scientific knowledge which would enable him to outclass his contemporaries. In 1877 he designed the catamaran *Amaryllis*, which was so innovative and so quick in a following wind that the little multi-hulls built in her image were soon disqualified by all the ruling bodies. Never mind: in 1878 Nat Herreshoff set up his own yard in Bristol, the Herreshoff Manufacturing Company, with his brother John Brown Herreshoff, who by then was blind.

Nat Herreshoff proved just as capable at designing mono-hulls. He designed them light and fast, made to glide over the water, and it was he who had the idea of separating the rudder from the keel. He was also one of the first to design yachts with a much smaller displacement, and he invented the modern sailing dinghy, which relies entirely on the weight of the crew for its stability. Racing rules, more anxious to preserve the existing fleet than to favor progress, were a constant barrier to him.

A keen advocate, before his time, of speed through lightness and innovation, Nat Herreshoff paradoxically made

OPPOSITE
Mariette *or the classic elegance of a Herreshoff design. The Wizard of Bristol was an expert at designing and building yachts that were at the same time both beautiful and fast.*

PAGES 66–7
Mariette *sailing close-hauled in an east wind on an overcast day in the bay of Saint-Tropez. The deck is in turmoil as the crew prepares to move round the cockpit while easing out the sails.*

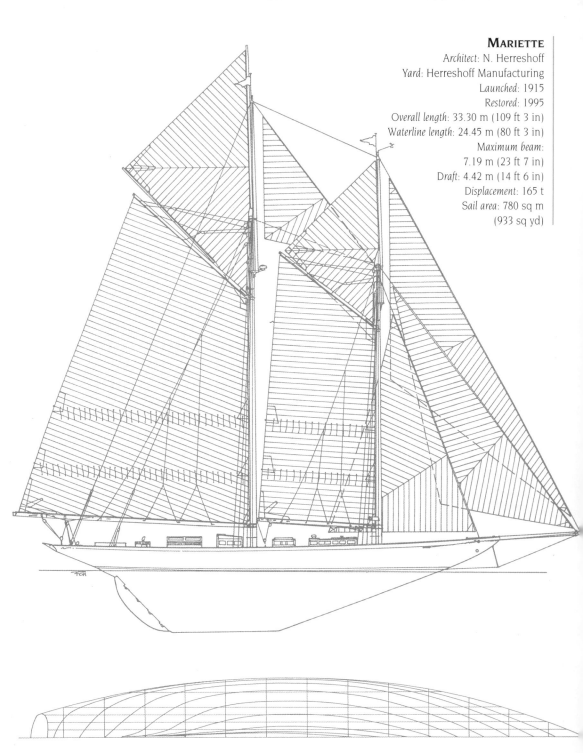

## MARIETTE

Architect: N. Herreshoff
Yard: Herreshoff Manufacturing
Launched: 1915
Restored: 1995
Overall length: 33.30 m (109 ft 3 in)
Waterline length: 24.45 m (80 ft 3 in)
Maximum beam:
7.19 m (23 ft 7 in)
Draft: 4.42 m (14 ft 6 in)
Displacement: 165 t
Sail area: 780 sq m
(933 sq yd)

history as the designer of much heavier, bigger boats that were also much faster. He designed and constructed *Reliance*, one of the most fantastic sailing vessels of all time. With a sail area of 1,500 sq m (1,800 sq yd), a length of 63 m (207 ft), a single mast, a crew of sixty-four men, and a boom which itself measured more than 43 m (141 ft) and served a mainsail weighing four tons, *Reliance* was the boat that took all the superlatives. The boom for the spinnaker was more than 25 m (82 ft) long and the winches, also designed by Herreshoff, were such jewels of avant-gardism that they were reutilized up until 1937 aboard J-class boats. Nat Herreshoff was also involved with the adoption in 1906 of international standards which have had such an influence on the history and development of yachting.

In 1915, to command a Herreshoff boat meant appealing to the most imaginative mind of the era. To have it built in his yard gave one the privilege of having a boat made with the most advanced techniques of the day. The Boston owner Frederick J. Brown had no hesitation in going down this road for his schooner *Mariette*. Launched in 1915, she is one of a famous line of cruiser–racers, the most celebrated being *Westward*, *Ingomar*, and *Vagrant*, which belonged to Harold Vanderbilt, the owner of the J-class *Ranger* that won the America's Cup in 1937. *Mariette* was utilized by Frederick Brown for ten years, until 1927. Her new owner, Francis Keno Crowninshield, rechristened her *Cleopatra's Barge* II in memory of a boat built by his ancestors in 1816. He kept her until 1941, when the US Navy requisitioned her and turned her into a coastal patrol boat.

The post-war years saw *Mariette* pass through many hands, being successively renamed *Gee Gee* IV and *Janeen*, doing time as a charter boat in the Caribbean, out of St. Lucia, and being owned in turn by Canadians and Swiss. Things became steadier from 1979, when the Italian publisher Alberto Rizzoli acquired her, gave her back her original name and sent her in for a serious overhaul, concentrating on the interior arrangements, at the Beconcini yard in La Spezia. He then took her on cruises around the Mediterranean, and sailed her in the first classic rallies in the mid-1980s.

*Mariette* was not to undergo her major refit until 1995, when a new American owner, Tom Perkins, decided to restore her to a luster that would match that of the most beautiful classic yachts around. The work was based on the boat's original plans, supplied by the Massachusetts Institute

of Technology, the very school where Nat Herreshoff had studied. The plans made it possible for Tom Eaton, former skipper of the famous Alden schooner *Puritan* and leader of the restoration project, to recreate, with the aid of the British rigger Harry Spencer, the sail plan and masts in their original configuration. The operation was carried out at the Beconcini yard in 1995, and was also a chance to give the interior arrangements some of their original glory by means of numerous modifications directed mainly at returning her more closely to her appearance at the time of her launch.

Since her rebirth, *Mariette* has been out racing and has made use of her newfound potential to monopolize capturing the trophies. She is crewed by a team of exceptional quality who set out to win, although that kind of spirit may not always have been present on the classic yacht circuit.

These boats are, above all else, exceptional objects which must be preserved, and racing is for most of them just an opportunity to sail well and be seen. It was bad luck that *Mariette* was involved in the regrettable accident at the Nioulargue in 1996 which resulted in the death of a crewman on the other boat, the six-meter *Taos Brett* IV.

OPPOSITE
Luxury, calm, and sensual pleasure: detail of the bell engraved with the boat's name; the outdoor saloon, set up when Mariette is at her moorings; the companionway and aft gangway; and the central saloon.

ABOVE RIGHT
Mariette *under full sail in the Mediterranean.*

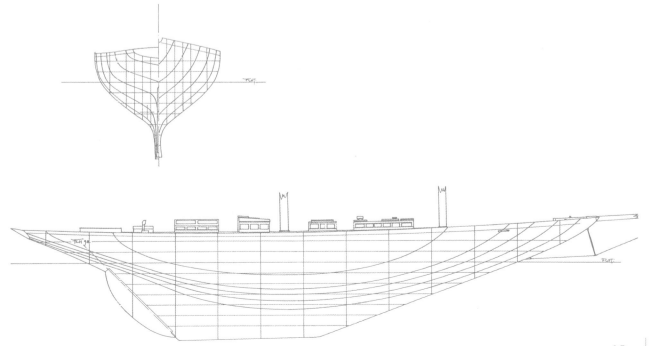

RIGHT
When reaching, and if the wind is strong enough, the crew lets out an asymmetrical spinnaker and a staysail between the two masts to increase the sail area.

The accident rather tarnished the image of a boat which nevertheless remains an absolutely magnificent yacht, and one of those which has traveled the most miles in just a few seasons. She was seen, for example, in 1997, in the great New York to Southampton transatlantic race which pitted classic yachts against each other, then in the rallies in the Mediterranean the following summer, in the Caribbean once more during the winter of 1998, then back in the Mediterranean. *Mariette* sails well and strongly. Time and distance will hopefully erase the bad memories of that gray day in October 1996.

BELOW
*Crewed by a team of professional regatta sailors, Mariette crosses oceans to join races in both Europe and America.*

# 8-m class

8-M CLASS
## The jewels of
## the regatta

The ideal size for a boat, whether it is old, new, a racer, or a cruiser, is a much-discussed topic. If she is too small, the elements, the wind, sea, and waves, soon remind us that a little extra length would not go amiss. If she is too big, problems are infinitely multiplied: costs, crew, the effort needed, the sail area, and the congestion aboard. So, when it comes down to defining the ideal size, people often agree on a "portmanteau" length of 10–15 meters (33–49 ft) — in other words the size of an eight-meter class.

Eight-meter class — what a barbaric name for such pretty boats! The term "eight-meter class" actually refers not to the length of the boat, which is usually about 14 meters (46 ft), but to a category of boat which conforms to the requirements of the international standard. What the chieftains of yachting created at their conference in London in 1906 was not a measure to allow boats of different sizes to race together, but a measure to define classes of boats that were very similar so that they could be fairly matched over a course in real time. The first result of the international conference — which put a number of existing boats out of the running — was to create classes for 5 m, 6 m, 7 m, 8 m, 9 m, 10 m, 12 m (the ones that contested the America's Cup until 1987!), 15 m (the size of *Moonbeam* and *Tuiga*), 19 m, and 23 m. It was a true revolution, leading to the creation of some magnificent boats, all very solidly built to Lloyd's specifications. After World War I there was a second major conference, which corrected some imperfections in the first version and reduced the number of official categories. Meanwhile, the eight-meter boats had enjoyed great success, as they were very close to the ideal size. Today, a few pioneers of the class are still sailing and delighting their owners, crews, and the public with their smoothness on the water and the purity of their lines.

Take *Estérel* — anyone would love to go offshore

OPPOSITE
*Aile VI crosses in front of the prow of Fulmar. The eight-meter class boats are principally small regatta boats with fairly basic interior arrangements. They sail well close to the wind and enjoy some very closely fought duels.*

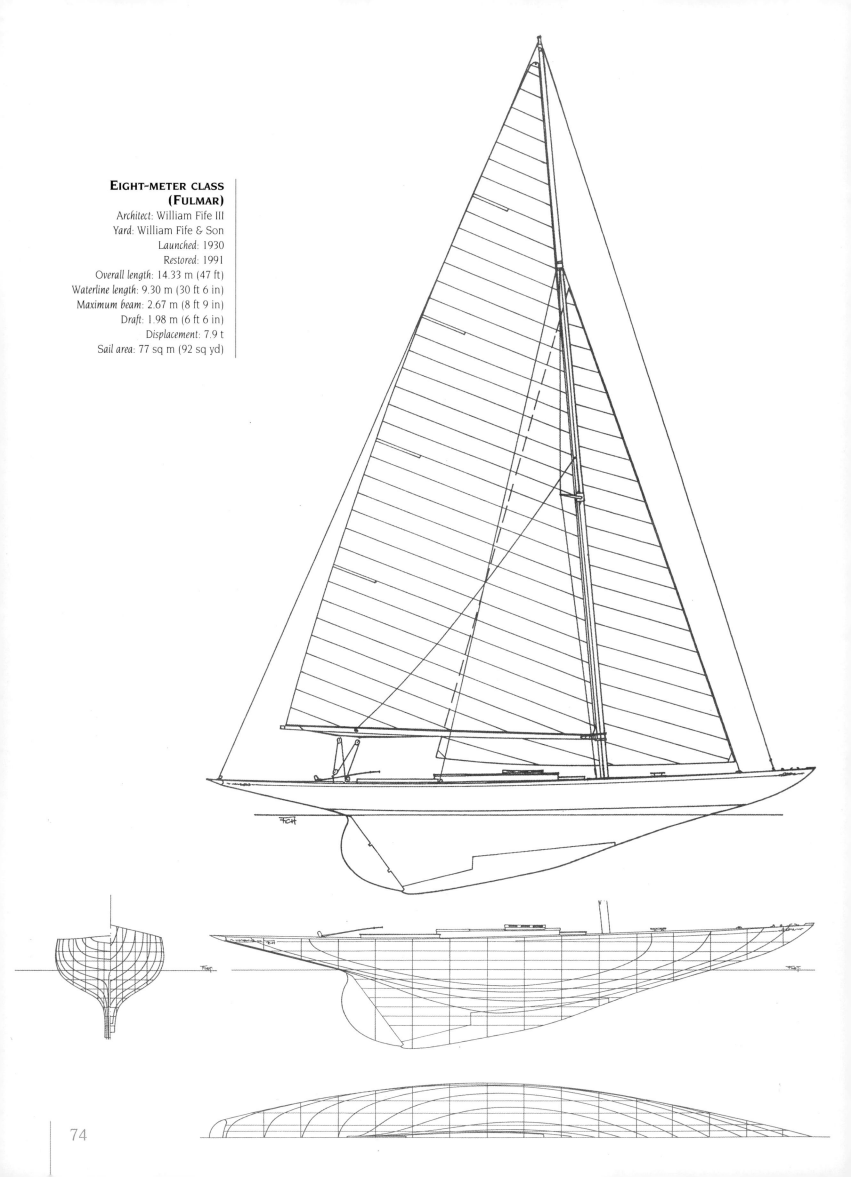

**EIGHT-METER CLASS
(FULMAR)**
Architect: William Fife III
Yard: William Fife & Son
Launched: 1930
Restored: 1991
Overall length: 14.33 m (47 ft)
Waterline length: 9.30 m (30 ft 6 in)
Maximum beam: 2.67 m (8 ft 9 in)
Draft: 1.98 m (6 ft 6 in)
Displacement: 7.9 t
Sail area: 77 sq m (92 sq yd)

Take Estérel — anyone would love to go offshore aboard such a pretty little boat! Her resurrection was something of a miracle. She was languishing in a corner of the Vieux-Port in Marseilles when Patrick Williamson, the driving force behind a local shipyard, succeeded in putting together a syndicate of owners to buy this hull which was heading fast for the breaker's yard. The restoration, carried out between 1990 and 1991, led to her being very much noticed at the Nioulargue, and later at the great rally in Brest in 1992. She had been entrusted to Sébastien Grall, a marine carpenter with much tact and good taste, who did a superb job right there in Marseilles. Many years before, it had been a French architect — Léon Sabille, also from Marseilles — who had drawn the plans for this boat. She was originally built in Marseilles in 1912, at a time when big sails of the Bermuda type had not yet appeared. She therefore sports a gaff rig which gives her a lot of presence combined with an incomparably roguish air.

Fulmar, launched in 1930, has had a much more traveled existence, having stagnated for some ten years on a Canadian mudbank before being restored to life in 1991. Born with the name Oonah, from a design by William Fife III, she was the champion of the Clyde in 1934, 1935, and 1936. Originally ordered by an Englishman in 1929, it seems she remained in Scotland because of trouble over her payment.

LEFT
Details of the tiller and of the mainsheet of the Fife-designed Fulmar. As with all classic yachts, you have to take off your shoes when you go aboard to avoid soiling or damaging the deck.

Brought back to Europe from Canada, Fulmar benefited from the best possible treatment as her restoration was entrusted to the expert hands of Duncan Walker and his team at Fairlie Restorations. The completed work is close to perfection. Fulmar has never had a motor, her deck layout is one of absolute purity, having never been fitted with winches, and some items have been recast to conform faithfully with the original plans, which have notes on them in the architect's own hand. The interior, although perfectly sober, is a model of cabinetmaking that is almost a masterpiece. It is such a pleasure once more to see this very simple and perfect boat sailing against her old rivals.

Aile VI, another eight-meter boat on the classic circuit, did not have to wait for restoration to enjoy her hour of glory. She belonged to a woman, and what a woman! Virginie Hériot was a rich heiress who might have been satisfied with the life of a grande bourgeoise, but the sea was her passion. She owned no fewer than eleven different boats and sailed tirelessly in regattas — so much so that in British circles she was known as the "queen of yachting." Not only was she was one of the rare women to win her stripes as a

RIGHT
Aile VI, *one of*
*Virginie Hériot's*
*boats, will go down in*
*history for winning a*
*gold medal at the*
*1928 Olympic*
*Games.*

OPPOSITE
*In a breeze, eight-*
*meter boats almost*
*turn into submarines*
*and are not always*
*easy to sail, especially*
*on a reach when they*
*start rolling.*

PAGES 78–9
*The virginal purity of*
*an eight-meter boat*
*— Fulmar, sailing*
*close-hauled.*

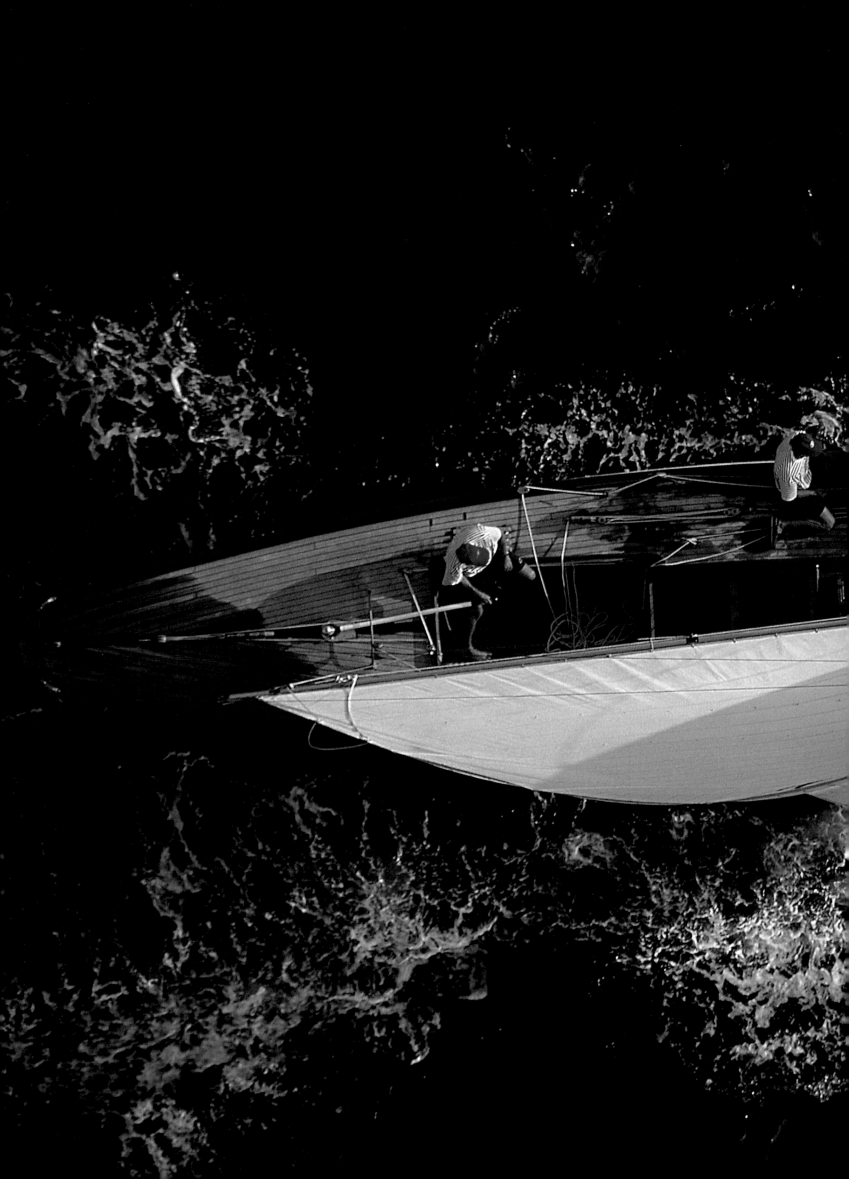

skipper in the ultimately very masculine world of yachtsmen and yacht clubs, but she was also bold enough to be a winner and carry off prizes at regattas. She had *Aile* VI built with the aim of regaining the French Cup on English territory in 1929 — which she did. In the meantime she had been selected for the 1928 Olympic Games in Amsterdam. She won a gold medal and the Italian Cup, which caused quite a stir at the time. Unfortunately she became ill and died in 1932 when she was only 42.

*Aile* VI was sold and sank into anonymity in the Mediterranean, where she passed through several owners, including a nautical club run by the French Navy in Toulon. She was saved at the last moment from being broken up by one of her greatest enthusiasts, François Tulan, and an application was made to have her classified as a historic monument. Then, in 1989, she was bought by the architect Philippe Briand. Unable to complete her restoration properly, he finally sold her to a group of owners who shared a passion for beautiful boats and for the Île de Noirmoutier in the Bay of Biscay. Her restoration was entrusted to Charpentiers Réunis of Cancale in northern Brittany, who put in 4,200 hours' work to give *Aile* VI back her original appearance and make her fit again to contest the strains of eight-meter class racing. Eighty percent of the boat had to be remade. In particular, the yard showed remarkable ingenuity in the way they managed to retain the planking intact while changing the boat's structural elements. The rigging was redesigned by the architect Guy Ribadeau Dumas, and the result is remarkable. Back on the circuit once more, racing against her old classic rivals in the eight-meter class, *Aile* VI proved just as efficient as she had been in the early days. All that was missing was the small silhouette of that great lady, invariably wearing a beret, who had first brought the yacht into being.

OPPOSITE
*The roguish elegance of the gaff-rigged eight-meter* Estérel, *which was designed, built and later restored in Marseille, where she is still based.*

ABOVE
*Aboard* Fulmar *you haul on the jib with the help of a hoist. When she is heeling, the cockpit is perilously near the water ...*

# Monaco Classic Week

The rallies of motor boats in Monaco at the beginning of the twentieth century were a major event for anyone interested in the latest technical advances. There you could admire great spluttering monsters trying to reach crazy speeds.

Strange-shaped hulls, which had trouble staying still when they stopped, were propelled by enormous motors bent on exploding. The *mille lancé* ("one-mile dash") was the ultimate challenge — the stuff of dreams for those who, from the very beginnings of airplanes and automobiles, were committed to the future of the combustion engine. Here people saw the appearance of the first hydrofoils, the first trimarans, and also a few hydroplanes which were still not entirely reliable.

## At the start of the twentieth century

The first rally was organized in 1904, and was inspired by Fernand Blanc, then director of the Société des Bains de Mer (Sea Bathing Company). He had little difficulty in convincing the reigning prince, Albert I, who was an oceanographer and a committed yachtsman. This meeting was an immediate success, with crowds of 25,000–30,000 massing on the quaysides to see these terrifying monsters. People came from all over Europe and America to look at the latest inventions. These generally arrived by train, before being loaded onto carts to pass in procession before the astounded crowd. It was a tremendous time.

It is still going on. The city of Monaco has always honored the engineer. From Grand Prix races to car rallies, from offshore racing to gatherings of veteran and vintage cars, Monaco glows with the red of Ferrari, gleams with the sheen of the Rivas, and boasts more

super-yachts per square foot than any other port in the Mediterranean. It is therefore scarcely surprising that the idea of organizing a rally for boats should have reemerged, although with one essential difference: this time they would be boats which had become vintage models. The idea seemed all the more natural given that Prince Albert of Monaco presided over the destiny of the sumptuous Yacht Club nestling at the end of Quai Antoine I at the very foot of the famous rock.

During the course of September 1994, under the leadership of Bernard d'Alessandri, director of the Yacht Club, and in the tradition of the Ribbolzi Trophy which brought together a number of vintage motor boats, the Monaco Classic Week took off. Ever since that time, it has maintained its special status as one of the finest rallies on the classic yacht circuit. Monaco, on account of its peculiar climatic conditions, is not a place for regattas in the true sense of the word; the wind there is often weak and erratic. On the other hand, it is one of the most complete rallies because traditional sailing boats can

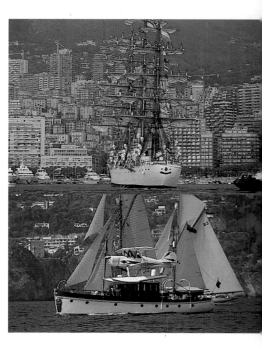

*ABOVE*
*Four-masters, classic yachts, hydroplanes, boats, and motor yachts — the Monaco Classic Week brings together sailing, motor, and even steam craft.*

*OPPOSITE*
*Perched on the yards of the Chilean three-master Gloria, cadets pay tribute to the Principality at the 1997 Monaco Classic Week, which closed the celebrations for the 700th anniversary of the Grimaldi dynasty.*

be seen side by side with vintage motor boats — two worlds which have their own customs and meeting places, and which very rarely have the opportunity to take part in a show together.

## Sailing boats and motor yachts

While the great traditional sailing boats and sumptuous motor yachts are moored at the Quai des États Unis, the small vintage motor boats are to be seen near the famous "swimming pool." After inspection by a jury, which closely scrutinizes their state of maintenance and the quality of their restoration, all the boats, both sailing and motor, put out to sea to take part in the various competitions. The *mille lancé*, which times the speed of motorized meteors between two buoys set one nautical mile (1.15 miles or 1.85 km) apart, has been restored to a place of honor, and several regattas are organized for the sailing boats.

The procession of boats entering the port is a superb theatrical spectacle. There you can see tiny steam boats passing with all sirens howling beneath the monumental bows of the three-masters, and racers from the golden age crossing the harbor in a burst of noise for a closer view of the traditional yachts embarked on a challenge race around three buoys.

In 1997, to mark the 700th anniversary of the Grimaldi dynasty, the parade brought together everything in the nautical world that could be called a boat: from the Russian four-master *Sedov* to the smallest vintage boat, via *Creole*, *Shenandoah*, and *Tuiga*, this whole boisterous and colorful world was out on the water, creating a huge celebration of the sea.

Monaco would not be Monaco if there was not a certain prestige attached to all that, and the evening which brought together owners and selected guests at the Sporting was the crowning event of the week. The occasion was distinguished by the presence of such sailing personalities as Juan Carlos, king of Spain, Éric Tabarly and the Swiss navigator Pierre Fehlmann.

Now well anchored in the traditional yachting season, the Monaco rally starts and finishes with an assembling regatta. The first one draws all the participants from Genoa or Imperia, while the second sends them off toward Cannes and its Royal Regattas — both of them inviting the yachts to cast off and head for new horizons.

*ABOVE AND BELOW RIGHT*
*Tremendous celebrations, with steamboats, period costume, spluttering launches, and people coming to Monaco to see and be seen, are just what is needed to create a sparkling occasion.*

*OPPOSITE*
*Sailing and motor yachts lined up along the Quai des États Unis.*

*RIGHT*
*Aboard the Argentinean three-master* **Libertad.**

*OPPOSITE*
*An early morning encounter on the open sea off Monaco.*

# KENTRA
## In search of lost time

"Mr. Livingston's yacht, I presume?" Absolutely. *Kentra* did in fact belong to Charles Livingston, an accomplished yachtsman from the first part of the twentieth century, who worked as a naval architect from time to time and was very active in the yachting scene around Liverpool, where he lived. So he had nothing to do with the famous nineteenth-century explorer David Livingstone. *Kentra* was actually Livingston's twenty-fifth and penultimate boat. It was a case of love at first sight when Charles Livingston, a member of the Royal Yacht Squadron, found her being built at Fife & Sons. He was seduced almost to the point of having a sister ship built, but in the end he waited, and it was some time before the boat of his dreams became available to him. The historian William Collier, a specialist in Fife boats, recounts that Livingston, having been informed of this by telegram, arrived the very next day with a check in his hand. For twelve years he was able to sail *Kentra* as much as he liked, and regularly took her sailing off the Scottish coast until advancing age forced him in 1936 to buy a smaller boat.

*Kentra* is a purely Scottish product, built by Scots for Scots — and for the first years of her life she also sailed in Scottish waters. Her first owner, Kenneth M. Clark, came from a family which had made its fortune in the manufacture of weaving looms, and retired from business at the age of 24. He owned sufficient land in Scotland to name his yacht for one of his estates — a small bay near Ardnamurchan on the west coast. He took possession of *Kentra* in 1923, but hardly used her and sold her on to Charles Livingston the following year. There are some owners whose chief pleasure comes from choosing an architect, working out the design with him, seeing the boat built, and then leaving the task of sailing and making use of it to others — which is a pleasure of a quite different sort.

*Kentra*, a gaff-rigged ketch, was never intended for racing, which explains her rather squat sail plan, divided into numerous sails of limited area which can thus be manipulated without too much effort. The same principle accounts for the absence of a staysail above the mizzen, the somewhat pug-nosed appearance of the bow, and her long overhanging stern, which would never have conformed to any racing standard.

OPPOSITE
*A strange encounter on Kentra's deck, where two little Scottish elves have secretly slipped on board!*

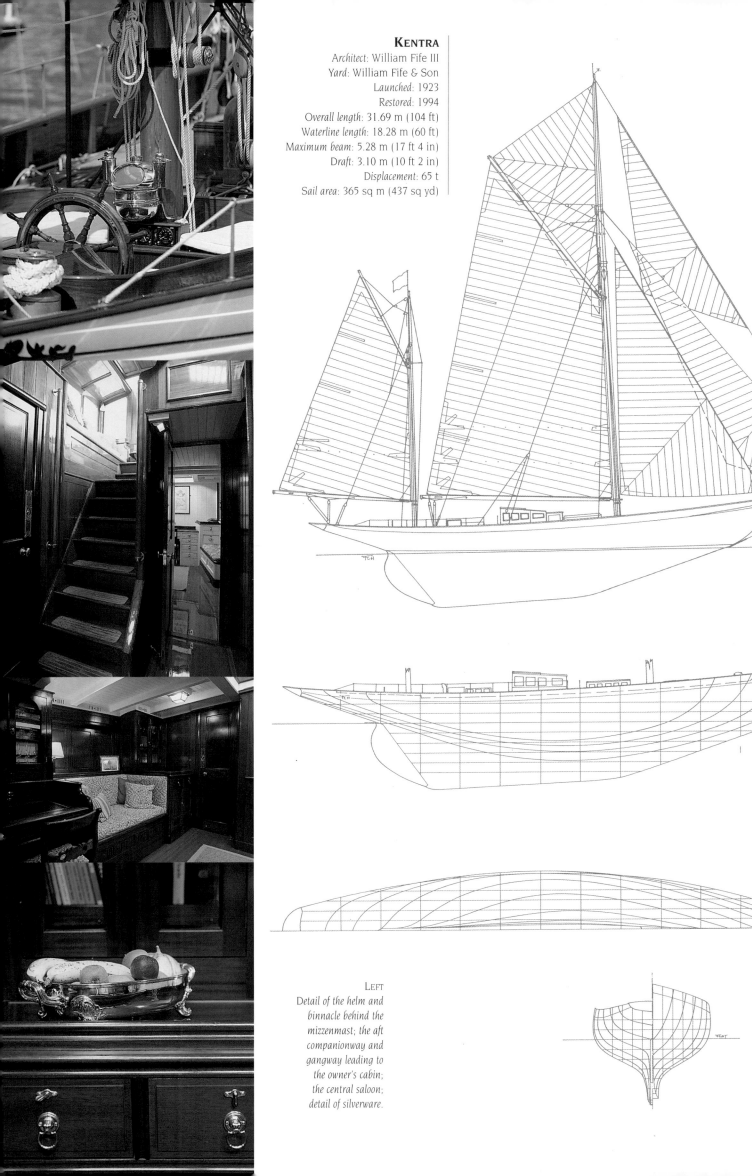

## KENTRA

Architect: William Fife III
Yard: William Fife & Son
Launched: 1923
Restored: 1994
Overall length: 31.69 m (104 ft)
Waterline length: 18.28 m (60 ft)
Maximum beam: 5.28 m (17 ft 4 in)
Draft: 3.10 m (10 ft 2 in)
Displacement: 65 t
Sail area: 365 sq m (437 sq yd)

LEFT
Detail of the helm and
binnacle behind the
mizzenmast; the aft
companionway and
gangway leading to
the owner's cabin;
the central saloon;
detail of silverware.

Charles Livingston's successor was a long way from the world of regattas, and indeed from sailing in general. Under the ownership of Barclay Hogarth, *Kentra* hardly ever left her moorings. He retained her until 1952, and then she found a new owner who did not keep her long. The subsequent owner was more attentive but, rather surprisingly, bought the boat without ever having seen her as she sailed in a flotilla towards southern England. For Major Charles Bassey Thorne, the idea of being able to handle this ketch with a small crew had a kind of primordial appeal — he immediately headed for the Mediterranean with only his wife and one sailor for company. *Kentra* had been given a Bermuda rig, which, apart from being more efficient, made her easier to maneuver — there was no peak to hoist. Based in the Balearic Islands, *Kentra* was used constantly by the Thornes for four years, and also as a charter vessel — which is how she became host to a number of well-known personalities such as Christina, Infanta of Spain, Errol Flynn, and Brigitte Bardot.

From 1958 to 1983, her owners changed at an accelerating rate, creating an increasingly urgent need for a total overhaul. She would have to wait almost ten years for this. Meanwhile, the unhealthy succession of owners produced many serious moments of uncertainty when it looked as if she might be abandoned altogether. So it is in the lives of vintage yachts. They have a period of dazzling glory and then sink slowly into inactivity and abandonment and being broken up or burned seems their most likely fate. But then, some time later, they always manage to get going again.

Not until 1990 did *Kentra* meet a patron who could give her back both life and hope. He was an American, and he wanted to have her restored in Scotland. Equipped with borrowed sails, she was escorted to the yard of McGruers at Gareloch near Glasgow, pulled onto dry land and stripped down. The project then came to a halt, complicated by a number of serious legal disputes.

But in 1993 another miracle occurred, this time for keeps, in the shape of a new Swiss owner. Following in the wake of *Altaïr*, *Tuiga* and company, the fashion for restorations was already widely established, and the taste for Fife designs was at its height, all of which proved be a godsend for *Kentra*. There was just one problem: the yard which would be doing the work, Fairlie Restorations, was located in the south of England, whereas *Kentra*, or the pieces that were left of her, was in Scotland. The remains of her hull were transported on a barge under the vigilant gaze of Harry Spencer who, apart from being unquestionably the right person when it came to restoring the rigging of a period yacht, seemed to be specially gifted in the field of high-risk transport for nautical marvels which were in a pitiful state and on the verge of total disintegration.

ABOVE
*Pressed by demanding owners, winch-makers produced items of modern gear in bronze, in keeping with the spirit of classic yachts.*

LEFT
*The décor in Kentra's aft cabin is delightful, and very much a part of the whole style of the interior arrangements.*

PAGES 92–3
*Kentra sailing close-hauled off Bénodet at the time of Pen Duick's centenary.*

However, with plenty of love and know-how, the impossible can always be achieved. Brought safely to harbor, *Kentra* was handed over to Duncan Walker and his team, who began by changing seventy percent of her ribs. The planking had to be partly renewed, but fortunately the interior regions were largely reusable. They were nevertheless improved with the most modern equipment, such as desalinators, electrical systems, and hydraulic power, which, after all, is not so far removed from the spirit in which the boat was built: to be able to sail easily with a small crew. One of the most difficult problems concerned the deck, where the original hoisting equipment was long gone. So they had to get out the original plans and cast new pieces in keeping with the boat's period.

Restored once more as a cruising yacht, and now based in Monaco, *Kentra* has since sailed hundreds of miles, crossed the Atlantic Ocean twice, been to regattas in the Mediterranean, and in 1998 made the pilgrimage to greet her elder sister *Pen Duick* and join her old rivals for the rally of Fife boats at Fairlie. It was all about making up for lost time, and gave proof, if proof were needed, that the most beautiful yachts are mainly the ones that do a lot of sailing.

OPPOSITE
*Detail of the compass.*
*In the old days, they*
*slipped a small oil*
*lamp into this housing*
*to illuminate the*
*compass rose during*
*the night watches.*

LEFT
*Even if she balks at*
*going to regattas,*
*Kentra has remained*
*committed to cruising*

95

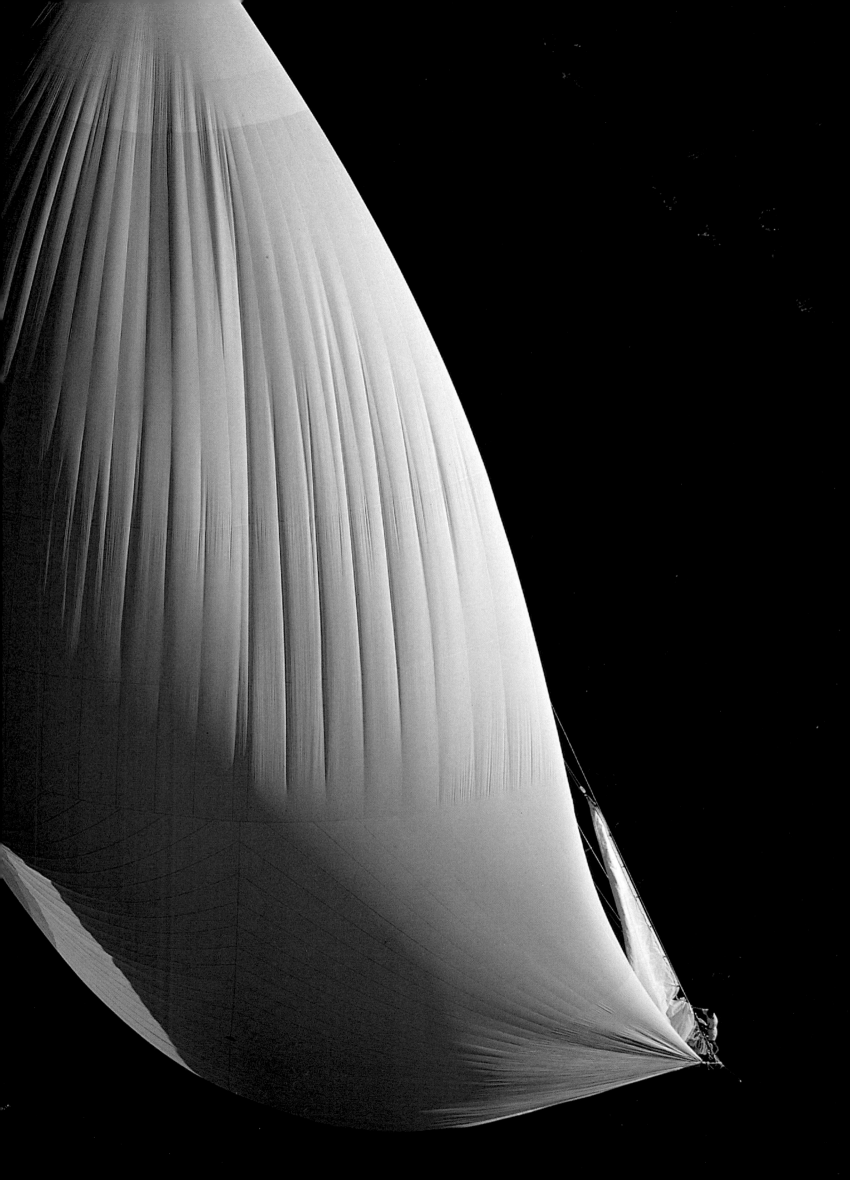

## CREOLE
## An extraordinary
## sailing ship

Certain phenomena, certain creations of the mind are so extraordinary, give rise to such intense emotions, and bring so much originality to their age, that they are called masterpieces. In the yachting world, *Creole* may well occupy this special position. Here is a boat outside all the norms of size, aesthetics, and history.

To see *Creole* sailing in a brisk breeze is a pleasure without equal. To come upon *Creole* secretly lying at anchor in the hollow of a sheltered bay opens the gates to the land of *A Thousand and One Nights*. Relaxed beneath her immense white rain awning, the beautiful schooner seems to pose there in heavenly perfection. Her long black hull, impeccably maintained, is an aesthetic wonder. Her rigging is very unusual, consisting of three equal-sized masts, and gives her a unique silhouette even in the narrow circle of large three-masted schooners. Her spoon-shaped bow, which seems so monumental from close up, cleaves neatly through the ocean waves separating hundreds of tons of water, equivalent to her displacement. The long slope of the transom seems never-ending, catching every ray of light and playing with the reflections that brush the letters of a name which is itself an invitation to everything that is exotic.

The designer of this great black schooner was British, and his name was Charles E. Nicholson. She was one of the last great cruising boats that he designed, and although he rather thought of her as his masterpiece, he was badly rewarded for his efforts.

She had been ordered by an American named Alec Smith Cochran, who wanted a very big cruiser which could still be maneuvered by a relatively small crew. Charles Nicholson put all his knowledge and inventiveness to work, and came up with this remarkable rigging — very original in its day — consisting of three masts of equal height supporting only triangular sails, and without a single spar needing to be raised. The interior arrangements were veritable apartments, as the huge and voluminous interior was to be occupied by only five cabins. The helmsman's position was unexpectedly raised up in the middle of the immense teak deck. The forward cabin contained the kitchens, the cabin in the center was a deck saloon, and the aft cabin was the navigation room. The technology employed was in the forefront of its day: two motors, two generators, an electric icebox, and central heating.

OPPOSITE
*With the wind aft of the beam, Creole's great white spinnaker completely conceals the boat (which is not exactly small). The crewman on the bowsprit gives an idea of the sail's mighty proportions.*

## CREOLE

Architect: C. E. Nicholson
Yard: Camper & Nicholson
Launched: 1927
Restored: 1983
Overall length: 58 m (190 ft 3 in)
Waterline length: 42.50 m (139 ft 5 in)
Maximum beam: 9.44 m (31 ft)
Draft: 5.35 m (11 ft)
Displacement: 525 t
Sail area: 1,040 sq m (1,244 sq yd)

ABOVE
Detail of the boom end
with its embossed
plaque bearing the
crest of the boat.
Creole is not a
racing boat and
sails on an even keel
most of the time,
though this makes her
no less impressive.

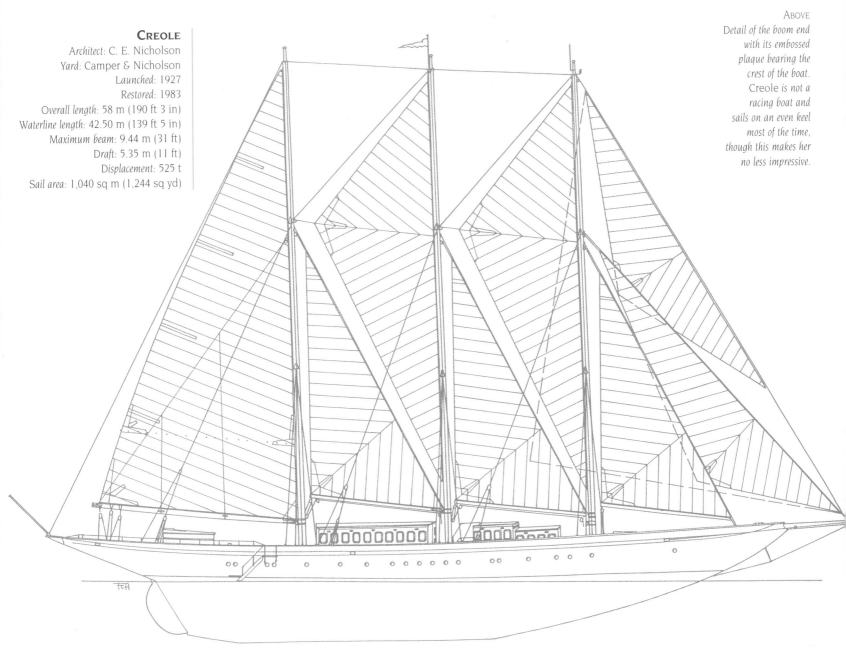

Unfortunately, the birth of this fabulous boat, christened *Vira* at her launch, suffered from that lack of understanding which sometimes arises between an owner and his architect. Even before she had sailed, the owner paid a visit to the Camper & Nicholson yard at Gosport in England and was terrified by the height of the masts. He asked for them to be shortened by ten feet (over three meters). Later he wanted another ten feet taken off, then ten more when the work was in progress. Charles Nicholson's fine rigging now made no sense at all! We can imagine his consternation, but that was not the last of his troubles. At the end of her first big cruise to the Mediterranean, Mr. Cochran complained that the boat was too heavy and uncomfortable at sea (mostly because she was carrying too much ballast for her sail area). Finally he agreed to his architect's advice to take out several tons of lead ballast. This operation was finally carried out in Spain, but the yard removed much more lead than they were asked to. In short, nothing went as planned.

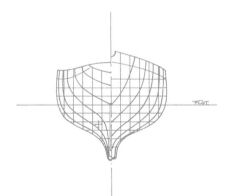

ABOVE
Creole's *black hull* needs a really special kind of maintenance as it catches the smallest ray of light. As with all the big boats, mooring beside a quay is a headache for the crew — usually they have to drop two anchors.

PAGES 100–101
All you need to see to work out the name of the boat — only Creole possesses such an extraordinary rigging.

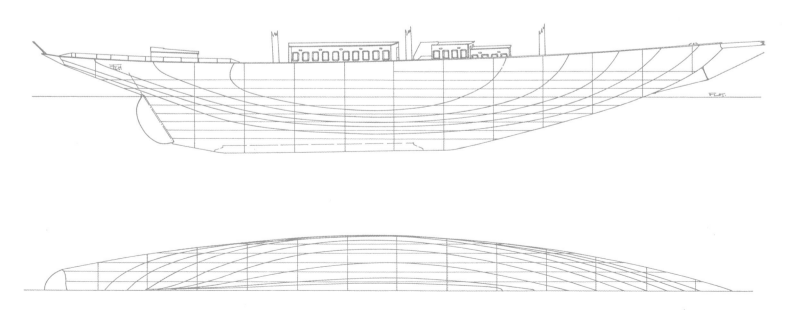

In 1928, following the death of her first owner, *Vira* was put up for sale. This substitute for a schooner (as she had become) was bought by Major Maurice Pope, a member of the Royal Yacht Squadron, who kept her, without making any modifications, until 1937. This was the year when Sir Connor Guthrie bought this wonder-boat with the intention of giving her the appearance and qualities that she deserved. He christened her *Creole*, and took her back to the yard so that her rigging and ballast could be put back into a proper shape and her lost honor restored.

A prestigious yacht once more, *Creole* resumed sailing, but the outbreak of war unfortunately brought an end to this first brief period of happiness. *Creole* suffered requisition and became a mine-hunter under the name of *Magic Circle*. She survived this dangerous role but was mastless when she was returned to the Guthrie family. Everything had to be done again, and indeed it was, for the next owner was Stavros Niarchos. The celebrated Greek millionaire took over the boat in 1948, fell in love with her, and laid his immense fortune at her feet. *Creole* was restored to her original shape at the German yard ISC. The great central coach became the owner's cabin, and air conditioning was installed so that he could display some of the numerous art masterpieces in his collection. The schooner became a veritable floating museum!

*Creole* was to receive many honors and retained her exalted status until 1970, the year Stavros Niarchos died. The beautiful schooner then plunged into a less sumptuous but more social existence, serving the Danish government as a rehabilitation center for young drug addicts. Then off she went again to the high life which was her right, now in the hands of the Italian industrialist Maurizio Gucci, who bought her in 1983. A dedicated yachtsman, passionate about sailing boats (he had supported the Italian challenge in the 1987 America's Cup), Maurizio Gucci restored the luster appropriate to a fine boat such as *Creole* and took her to rallies of traditional sailing craft. She sailed perfectly under the control of John Bardon, her skipper, displaying excellent form and sometimes consenting to slum it in regattas with other boats of her size, such as *Shenandoah* and *Adix*. When *Creole* goes by, time stops — and life becomes a dream as the beautiful schooner sails away to new horizons.

OPPOSITE
*Creole is, incontestably, one of the most beautiful boats in the world. However, this masterpiece by Charles Nicholson had to wait many years before she could benefit from the integrated rig of a three-masted schooner.*

ABOVE
*For Creole, a change of tack under sail in light winds generally means stopping altogether. But even going at a leisurely pace seems fitting for a yacht of this size. Once under way again, her superb bow wave speaks volumes for the smoothness of her hull.*

## DORADE

## A breath of fresh air

At the time of her launch, *Dorade* was a real revolution. Not only did this rather small, light, and sharp-looking yacht begin to hang around her more noble fellows she had been designed by a greenhorn, completely unknown at the time, named Olin Stephens.

It could be said that the two brothers Olin and Rod Stephens had forged themselves a reputation as passionate young regatta sailors on the Long Island Sound, the stretch of water local to New York City. But really they were mostly known at the Larchmont Yacht Club, which they often visited and where they had gotten into the habit of winning almost all the regatta prizes. Their father, Roderick Stephens, paid the bills and took much pleasure from seeing his two kids sailing with such fervor.

In 1920, the first family boat was a 4.24-meter Corker, followed by three other small sailing boats until, with their fifth family yacht, they finally acquired one equipped with a cabin. When Roderick became a member of the Larchmont Yacht Club, which was a very active organizer of international class regattas, notably in the six-meter class, Olin and Rod lost little time in becoming sought-after crew members. They took part in regattas beside the famous American skipper Sherman Hoyt, who won the America's Cup in 1934 at the helm of the J-class *Rainbow*.

The Stephens brothers finally convinced their father to buy a six-meter class. Their choice fell on *Natka*, which had never been highly placed until then, but which, in their hands, soon took off. In 1928, the Larchmont Yacht Club organized a design competition to create a boat which could serve as a workhorse for the junior members. Olin, who a short time previously had published his sketches for a six-meter class, was helped by Drake Sparkman, a New York yacht broker, who backed his project — and it won. This was the first boat bearing the signature Sparkman & Stephens, and marked the birth of one of the most formidable architects' practices of the twentieth century.

OPPOSITE
*This is the ventilation system invented by the Stephens brothers. It was so ingenious that it is now featured on most boats and is referred to as the "Dorade box." That was the name of the yawl the brothers designed and which drastically reshaped the design of ocean racers at the beginning of the 1930s.*

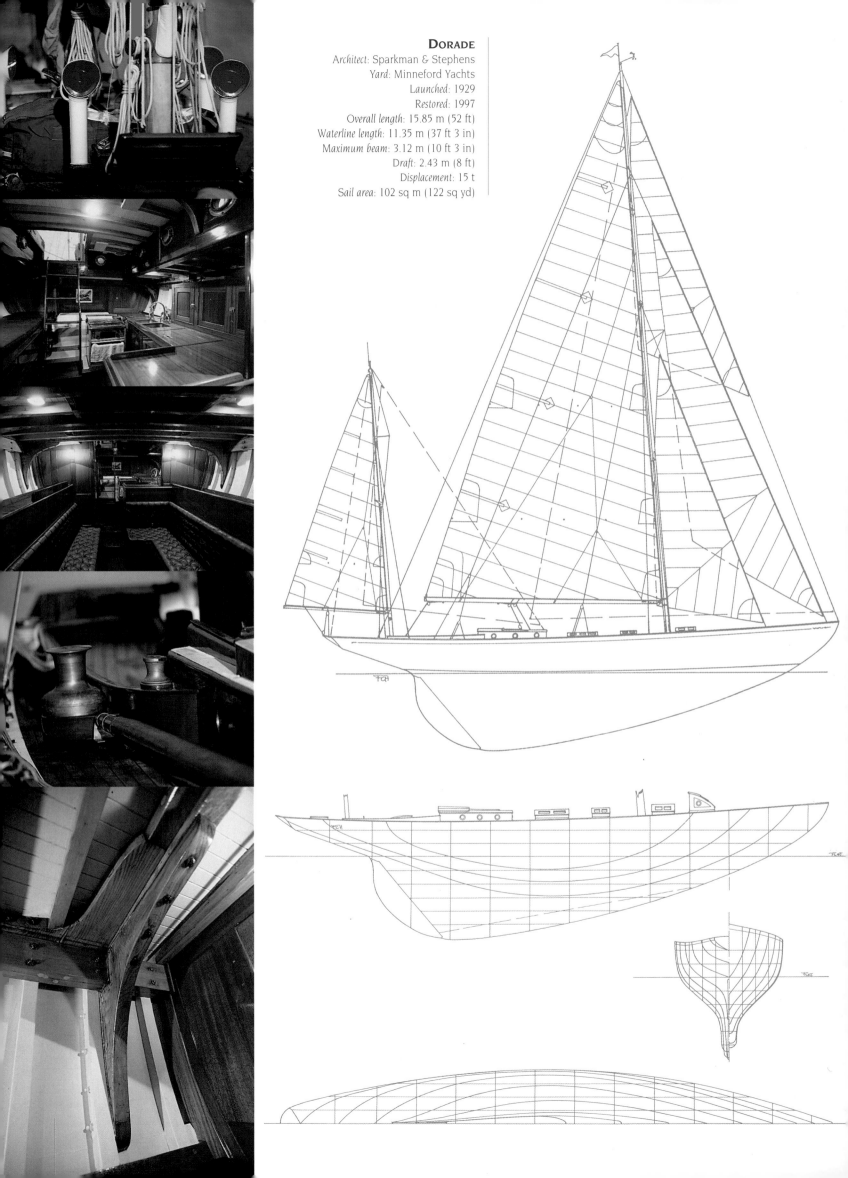

# DORADE

*Architect:* Sparkman & Stephens
*Yard:* Minneford Yachts
*Launched:* 1929
*Restored:* 1997
*Overall length:* 15.85 m (52 ft)
*Waterline length:* 11.35 m (37 ft 3 in)
*Maximum beam:* 3.12 m (10 ft 3 in)
*Draft:* 2.43 m (8 ft)
*Displacement:* 15 t
*Sail area:* 102 sq m (122 sq yd)

From six-meters to twelve-meters, from J-class to America's Cup winners, from victories in the Fastnet to others in the Admiral's Cup and the Whitbread, the name of Sparkman & Stephens soon became unbeatable in naval architecture circles. Olin made the designs, while Rod supervised the construction, taking passionate care with every detail of the deck and the rigging. The two Stephens brothers were also responsible for numerous cruisers and had a lot to do with the success of the famous Swan boats from the Finnish yard Nautor — those "Rolls Royces" of modern pleasure sailing. As the years went by, their practice became a nursery for many talented architects who would one day make it to the top — people like German Frers and Dave Pedrick. Few naval architects' offices have so dominated the art of designing champion racers over such a long period, but their careers really began with a marvelous little boat called Dorade.

Dorade was born very early on. She was number nine in the Sparkman & Stephens design book, and was designed in New York City, where Drake Sparkman had installed his protégé in a studio on City Island Avenue. Until then, Olin Stephens had designed only a few six-meter and eight-meter class boats. Dorade started a revolution in that she was no more than a large eight-meter boat expanded to compete in the open sea races that were the dream event for regatta people at that time. The owner, once more, was none other than Roderick Stephens himself.

At her launch in 1929, Dorade scared people. Too little freeboard, too small, too much sail, too narrow, too fragile, she also looked somewhat truncated because she lacked a bowsprit. She resembled an ugly duckling when set beside the monster boats of the day. They were real boats derived from fishing craft — they were broad, long, and heavy, with a high freeboard, and most of them bore the signature of the American architect John Alden.

In her very first competition, the Bermuda Race from Newport to Bermuda, Dorade finished third overall and second in her class, despite a navigating error. Regatta specialists were forced to take notice of this new concept in ocean racing boats. She was very close to the international class boats which were generally thought of as the thoroughbreds of their day. The following year, 1931, the two Stephens brothers, their father, and Sherman Hoyt raced across the Atlantic and left the other eight competitors far behind in their wake. It got even better: Dorade followed up by winning the Fastnet, which for the Stephens meant a heroic homecoming to the United States. Roderick then gave the boat to his sons who, the next year, won the Bermuda Race in the United States then the Fastnet in Britain/Ireland in 1933. Then they headed for the Pacific and the San Francisco–Honolulu, which they won in 1936 as well as many other American regattas in the meantime.

ABOVE
An uncompromising regatta craft, Dorade has remained an extremely efficient sailboat. Here at the helm is the restoration architect Doug Peterson.

OPPOSITE
Deck ventilators; view of the companionway and the galley aft; the central saloon; detail of the interior structure. Dorade is not a big boat, and was beautifully restored in 1997.

PAGES 108–9
You can understand why the nabobs of the day were frightened by this little boat, which seemed to them to be too short, too low in the water, too narrow, and carried too much sail compared to other boats around. Dorade was designed, however, to race on the open sea and was victorious in the major competitions in which she entered. She was a real little revolution.

When the Stephens brothers sold *Dorade* to a Californian in 1936, she had already proved a revolutionary boat. She would have other owners, enter other races, and go on other cruises. Gradually she disappeared from the front of the stage, but not without teaching her successors a thing or two. In order to ventilate the boat's interior better when sailing conditions were poor, the Stephens brothers thought up a kind of ventilation box with an air intake on top which allowed air to enter while keeping the sea spray out. This system, which could equally be sealed tightly in bad weather, was so ingenious that it was installed on other boats. and since then has been used aboard all the world's sailing boats under the name of the "*Dorade* box."

It was an emotional moment to see little *Dorade* reappear on the major rally circuit for traditional boats, at Porto Cervo in Sardinia in 1997. The boat had come through a very extensive restoration at the Italian Navy yard Argentario, which had also undertaken the refit of the twelve-meter class *Nyala*. They had had to take *Dorade* to pieces to work on the hull and the structure, and remake the deck as well as a large part of the interior arrangements — all in accordance with the original plans. Wherever possible, bronze hoisting equipment had been recovered, and the ventilation boxes, which had apparently been kept, were lovingly restored by the crew. As soon as she took up racing again, *Dorade* started winning regattas, just as she had done at the beginning.

*OPPOSITE*
*Designed around a hull directly inspired by international class boats, Dorade is a yawl rigged as a cutter — that is, with two masts, the mizzen being stepped aft of the steering gear, and two foresails. She has tremendous balance and efficiency.*

*LEFT*
*The random curves of the halyard, the marvelous wood, and the bronze deck gear with its patina gained from the thousands of miles the boat has logged*

## Lelantina
## Like a flying fish

It was at the Nioulargue in 1989. The mistral was blowing up a storm, and racing was cancelled for the day, which otherwise had been magnificent. Most of the boats stayed in the harbor, while their crews went off on various jaunts, but when the wind decreased at the beginning of the afternoon, some of the crews, including that of the beautiful schooner *Lelantina*, took a chance and went for a sail in the Gulf of Saint-Tropez. Suddenly, with hardly any warning, the mistral again unleashed its treacherous gusts. Surprised in all her pomp, *Lelantina* bent her spine, dipped her bulwarks in the water, and her wake churned out in a straight line across the gulf — magnificent!

It is unlikely that the wake of the schooner which, in effect, was the mother of *Lelantina* would have been quite so straight! *Lelantina* is actually the improved version of an Alden-designed schooner called *Lelanta*, which was launched in 1929. She was commissioned by an American named Ralph Peverley from John Alden, one of the most productive naval architects of the first half of the twentieth century. She was his 448th creation and was built at the De Vries shipyard in the Netherlands.

In her early life she performed respectably, notably at the 1930 Fastnet Race, which she was unfortunately forced to abandon after receiving heavy punishment in a violent burst of wind. The magical proportions of her schooner rig had prompted the renowned sailor and nautical writer Uffa Fox to comment: "The combination of sails which can be raised on this boat, from a flat calm to a burst of wind, is better than any other rig I know." These qualities did not prevent Ralph Peverley from feeling a little cramped aboard his boat. So he decided to commission the same schooner from John Alden, but in a larger size, and that is how *Lelanta* II came into being in 1937; a few years later she became *Lelantina*.

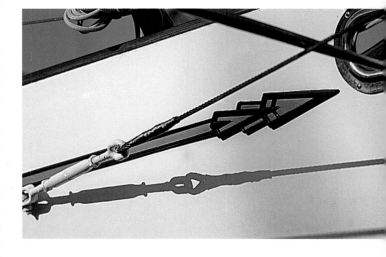

OPPOSITE
*Here is a boat that sails with surprising ease. Always there, always ready,* Lelantina *pirouettes on the water, and enjoys a gust as much as a light breeze. She is a real flying fish.*

ABOVE
*Details of a ventilation hatch, fittings on the mast, and the small outside cockpit.*

OPPOSITE ABOVE
*The cabins and saloon in a version which has since been improved upon.*

PAGES 116–17
*Plunging into waves raised by a strong east wind, Lelantina revels in her situation — the crewman in the bow is not so keen perhaps.*

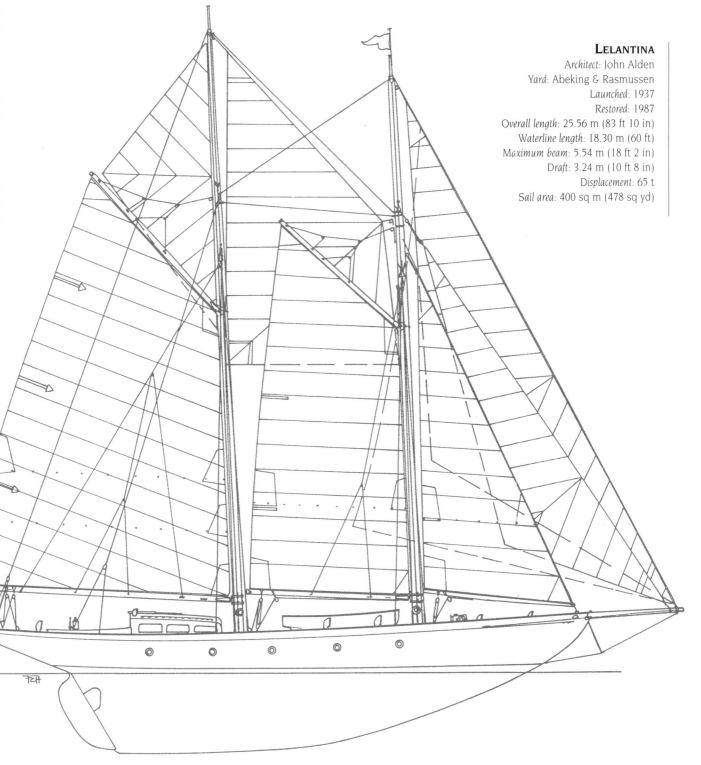

## LELANTINA

*Architect:* John Alden
*Yard:* Abeking & Rasmussen
*Launched:* 1937
*Restored:* 1987
*Overall length:* 25.56 m (83 ft 10 in)
*Waterline length:* 18.30 m (60 ft)
*Maximum beam:* 5.54 m (18 ft 2 in)
*Draft:* 3.24 m (10 ft 8 in)
*Displacement:* 65 t
*Sail area:* 400 sq m (478 sq yd)

The mother boat lived her own life. She passed from hand to hand, even crossing the Atlantic to Brittany, where Gwenaël Bolloré put her to work on lobster-watching missions, and also as part of the setting for a film in which his wife was the lead actress. The boat suffered a quite scandalous setback when the sheriff of Naples, Florida, seized her in the act of drug smuggling; she had been deserted a few minutes previously by her shameful occupants, who had abandoned seven tons of marijuana in her hold!

*Lelantina* had a much more moderate life. The lines of her mother could not have been far from perfection, since the plans of the two boats are, apart from their proportions, interchangeable. Compared with John Alden's previous boats, notably the famous *Puritan*, the two *Lelantas* were a little finer in the stern and a little fuller in the bows, with the waterline slightly more extended.

For *Lelanta* II — alias *Lelantina* — Ralph Peverley sought only perfection. The yard chosen had to be masters in metal construction, for the boat's impeccable shape had to be wrought from riveted mild steel. The choice was a radical one: Abeking & Rasmussen, a yard extremely well versed in the leading technologies of the period when they had specialized in the construction of German U-boats!

The state of the hull today proves the rightness of this choice. The two masts made of spruce are the original ones, and stand out like leading men when, without moving a muscle, they have to put up with the indignities imposed by the high jinks of the Nioulargue.

In 1987, only the deck had to be entirely remade, though the interior arrangements are also not original. Purists may no doubt be offended by this, but the clients who have the chance to hire this yacht, so smooth and pure in form, would certainly not share their opinion. Unlike most vintage yachts, she has no partitioning to inhibit the feeling of space in the vast central area, which links the saloon, the dining area and the corner galley. The fine companionway, flanked by a mahogany banister, is the very heart of the boat and clears a view toward the deckhouse, which then becomes a split-level saloon like a mezzanine. The blending of different woods, from teak to pale pine and mahogany, produces a decorative scheme of incomparable warmth. Thus *Lelantina* succeeds in marrying a spatial concept, which might be called contemporary, with a very classical and traditional decorative style.

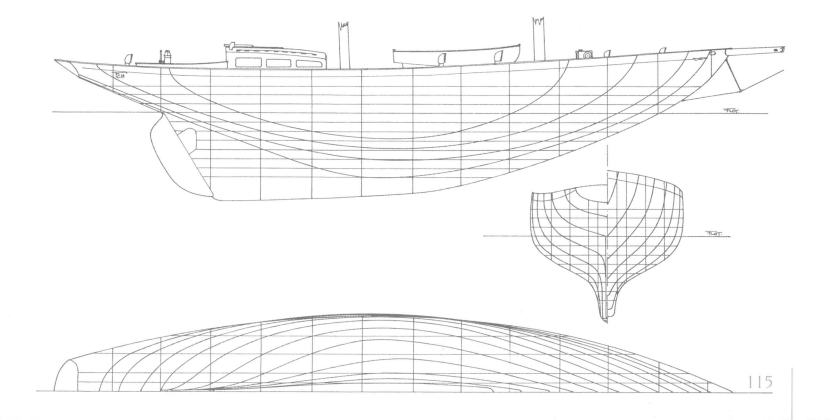

Ever since classic yachts began to be renovated, *Lelantina* has put her qualities to good use, becoming one of the most-sailed boats and deriving most of her means from the charter business. She was based for a long time in the Mediterranean but has also been seen in the Caribbean; she often attends regattas for much more modern boats, and she goes to all the rallies for traditional yachts. For day trips she can accommodate around thirty people, and for more private use she has space for eight guests to share the four charming cabins on board. Three of these have double couchettes, while the forward starboard cabin has two bunk beds. The decoration is simple but the detailing is fine. Philippe Lechevallier, her skipper for many years, has spent a massive amount of energy in finding items like the right period lamp, and in working on all the slightest details to ensure that his yacht remains faithful in every respect to the etiquette required by the history of yachting. Thanks to the many hours he has spent rummaging in antique shops, *Lelantina* has undoubtedly become a superb specimen.

The on-deck scene is a miracle of clarity. To walk barefoot along the great expanse of teak is a real pleasure, as it is to settle into the cushions of the small cockpit aft. One might wonder how such a sophisticated rigging can be managed with so few lines and deck fittings. Her elegance is certainly the reason she can be so easily maneuvered. The crew numbers no more than four, and that is enough to handle all the sails as easily as on a more modern sailboat.

Under sail, *Lelantina* is a model of smoothness and balance. The perfection of her silhouette is equaled only by her power and stability of line. Agile, alert, able to turn a light breeze immediately into a means of acceleration, *Lelantina* is not one of those dinosaurs which need a force five to wake them up. Her seventy tons provide ample weight to support 400 square meters (478 square yards) of sail up to speeds of thirty knots. While many traditional sailing boats avoid a blast of wind, *Lelantina* loves a breeze and copes with all types of weather. She is a real sailing boat.

OPPOSITE AND ABOVE
*Designed by the American naval architect John Alden,* Lelantina *carries a lot of sail but is easy to maneuver by virtue of the unusual way the sail area is divided up, giving her good balance under sail and making her simpler to control with only a small crew.*

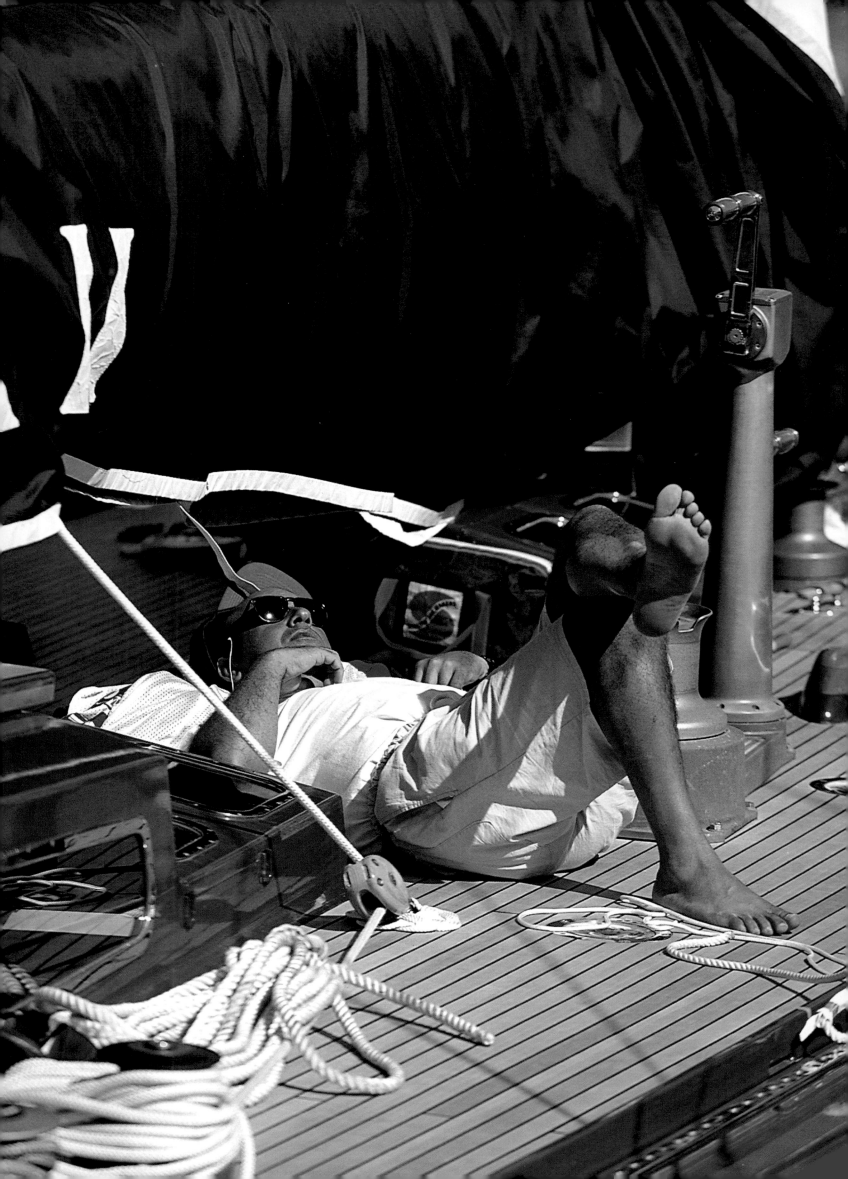

# Royal Cannes Regattas

**The Royal Cannes Regattas have a very special place in the annual circuit of classic yachts. Here people come principally to race.**

The essential considerations are these: set up a good crew, get a good start, sail the course well, round the buoys correctly, and try to get the best final placings so that you leave, if possible, with an armful of trophies.

Social occasions have a lower priority here than elsewhere, although they are of a very high standard. People take part in the Royal Cannes Regattas more for the sport than the parade. As the years have gone by, this spirit has become increasingly pervasive in the world of traditional yachting.

Obviously, bearing in mind the great age of the competing boats, it is not a matter of sailing in all weathers, or of pushing these venerable treasures to the limit — they soon cry out in pain when the wind and the sea get too strong. In the heat of the action, skippers have to remain calm and generally contain any aggressive feelings so that they stay within the limits and avoid collisions and the dreaded sound of breaking wood.

## An ideal stretch of water

The organizing committee of the Cannes Yacht Club, masterfully led for many years by Jean-Pierre Odero, knows its limits in the art of organizing races. However, it has the good fortune to possess a stretch of water perfectly suited to the event. In the third week of September, sailing conditions between the Îles de Lérins and the mountains of the Estérel are, for most of the time, very easy, with blue skies, flat seas, and gentle breezes at the end of the day. At other times, things may not be so great. People still remember the day on the Croisette when several municipal buses were summoned to protect the tented village, where the tents were threatening to fly off to Italy under the frantic assaults of a mistral gone crazy.

The other essential characteristic of the Royal Regattas is that this is the oldest of the rallies for racing sailboats. Since the birth of yachting, Cannes has benefited from the presence on its shores of wealthy owners who quickly learned to enjoy sailing close to their sumptuous holiday residences. The Société des Régates de Cannes was founded in January 1860 by Léopold Bucquet and Lord Bugham. Regattas were organized from 1863 and the Yacht Club itself was founded in 1867. The International Cannes Regattas, as they were then known, were organized for the first time in 1906.

*ABOVE*
*The lively Rue du Suquet seen in the beautiful evening light after the yachts have returned to harbor.*

*OPPOSITE*
*Racing is fine, but it doesn't stop you enjoying the wonderful Cannes sunshine.*

*LEFT*
**Altaïr** *and* **Thendara** *cross the bows of* **Shenandoah** *in the Bay of Cannes.*

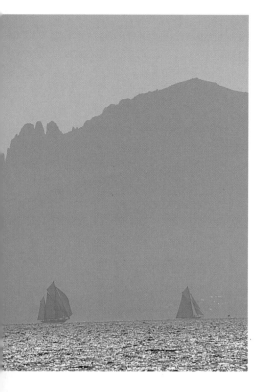

The event grew steadily until King Christian X of Denmark began to take part enthusiastically at the helm of his six-meter class *Dana*. Such an honor could not go without some acknowledgment, and that is how the Cannes regattas became Royal.

### The reasons for success

Since they resumed after two world wars, and despite an interruption from 1963 to 1974, the Royal Regattas have attracted a special kind of following: it consists mainly of foreign teams sailing in small classic one-design classes like *Dragon* and *Requin*, and six-meter and eight-meter class boats. These always make up the bulk of the competitors. And while other regattas have been eager to attract modern boats, the organizers at Cannes have preferred to favor owners over sponsored sailing. They have managed to welcome these crews and show off their boats to good advantage, even though they may be a shade old-fashioned. The climate and the quality of life on the Côte-d'Azur have done the rest, and the recipe still works well today. In Cannes, as well as taking part in some very well-heeled racing events, visitors can spend a pleasant week before the winter weather sets in. There are always a lot of foreign crews — German, Swiss, Swedish, Danish, and Norwegian — who do their best to come back year after year.

*ABOVE, RIGHT AND BELOW*
*Sailing quietly beneath the mountains of the Estérel; reading the chart while waiting for the wind; lucky spectators on the sea wall; getting tangled up in the spinnaker — this is Cannes in September, and it is very pleasant.*

*OPPOSITE*
*Thendara passes under the bow of a cruise liner at anchor — a sight you can see from back on the Croisette.*

*PAGES 124–5*
*Huddled beneath the old part of Cannes, the classic yachts have found a nest which suits them, even if getting out to sea and coming back from a race is a real headache for both helmsmen and organizers. The big yachts have to be almost shoe-horned in.*

*Pages 126–7*
*An eight-meter class race — at last a stiff breeze has arrived.*

For their greater comfort, the boats are moored beneath the old quarter in Cannes, and you only have to walk a few yards to reach your table in a good restaurant, or to find yourself leaning on the counter in some typical Mediterranean bar.

As the years have gone by, some twelve-meter class yachts have come to join the party, which is so perfectly suited to their delicate outlines.

Then, gradually, traditional yachts started to arrive in the harbor, which is such a natural stopover between the Italian rallies and the Nioulargue in Saint-Tropez — each year they grow bigger, more numerous, and more beautiful than ever. Finally, the big yachts started racing and competing, and more and more of them added the "Royals" to their diary for the following season.

Over the years, yet another element has added to the natural attractions of this regatta series: the Yacht Club de France Cup. This is the event which joins Cannes and Saint-Tropez, serving as a preview for the Nioulargue, and has become an indispensable link for yachting people who want to continue the party elsewhere. This splendid race over the twenty or so miles separating the two ports has become a fully fledged classic in which other more recent boats take part as a way of rounding off their vacation.

Sailing beneath the colorful slopes of the Estérel is a fine way of not having to say goodbye to your friends.

J-CLASS
# The giants of
# the crazy years

"J-class" is more than just a name, it's a concept. Attracting all the superlatives, it evokes images of gigantism, the crazy years of the 1930s, sailing with unlimited money, size, effort, weight, and power. Even today, J-class boats are the biggest and most prestigious racers in the world. Even if some older or more recent yachts are bigger than them in size, they do not benefit from the aura that surrounds the magic term "J-class." Few boats will have experienced the whirlwind of madness which drove their owners, at the height of an economic crisis, to invest ludicrous sums of money to have them designed and built. These were rare boats that reaped the benefits of so much architectural daring, of so many extreme technological solutions, to become the high-performance sailing craft of their age.

In all, ten J-class yachts were designed, all of them with the aim of winning the America's Cup in 1930, 1934 and 1937. Six were launched in America, four in England. All those built in the United States have today disappeared. Some were victims of their sophisticated construction, using alloys of chemically incompatible metals. Once surrounded by water, their hulls were transformed by means of electrolysis into a gigantic electric battery. Others were dismantled as part of the monumental American war effort. The English yachts, however, are still in existence.

Today, three of them are still sailing. *Shamrock V* was the first boat of Sir Thomas Lipton, the famous Irish tea merchant. She was based at Newport, on the East Coast of the United States. *Velsheda*, the most recent to be restored (in 1998), and *Endeavour*, the fastest, sail all over the world. In addition to these three J-class boats, which were conceived as such, there are three other racing boats of a similar size which were launched a few years earlier as 23-meter class yachts and were then adapted in various ways to fit with the J-class, which was created in 1928. These are *Cambria*, which nowadays lives in Australia, and *Candida* and *Astra*, which are based in the Mediterranean. Apart from *Cambria*, which is a Fife design, all these mighty boats were designed by Charles E. Nicholson and built at the Camper & Nicholson yard at Gosport, near Portsmouth, on the coast of southern England. All have been thoroughly restored in recent times, and occasionally sail against each other in classic regattas. Whenever they appear, the spectacle is breathtaking: such huge boats, such power, and such beauty too.

OPPOSITE
*Astra (J K-2) and Candida (K8) side by side, as they were when J-class yachts were the queens of the America's Cup. In fact, both these boats had to be hacked about to conform with J-class regulations, which only came into effect after they had been launched.*

ABOVE
*To maneuver a J-class requires plenty of effort and muscle power, and intelligence too, as the demands are massive and dangerous.*

*Astra*, the oldest of them all, was launched in 1928, commissioned by one of the great industrialists of the day, Sir Mortimer Singer, the king of electrical appliances. At times he could be a little outrageous in his approach to yachting (originally he wanted to own two J-class boats, one for sailing in light conditions, the other for breezy days), but he made no mistake when he ordered this great yacht from Camper & Nicholson. *Astra* was not a J-class to begin with, but a similar-sized boat corresponding to the international 23-meter class: she had an overall length of more than 35 meters and a sloop rig. She only raced in England for one season, in 1929, before her owner committed suicide (following a serious air accident). *Astra* only properly resumed racing with her third owner, Hugh Paul. He carried out the necessary modifications to the lower part of the hull and the sails so that she could be admitted to the new J-class, and she began racing in earnest in the 1930 season. Now she could show her true worth, and she won many races during the 1930s. After the war, she went to the Mediterranean, became Count Mattarazzi's cruiser, then was restored in 1984 by Antonio Buzzei at the Beconcini yard in La Spezia, Italy. Since then, *Astra* has sailed for the Gennaro family, who turned her back into a real racing yacht with an appropriate wardrobe of sails and, above all, a very tightly organized crew including several members accustomed to racing aboard entrants for the America's Cup!

*Candida*, launched barely a year after *Astra* in 1929, was built in the same style (composite hull with a steel keelson and mahogany fittings) for the British banker Herman Andreae. She was more slender than *Astra*, also beamier and with a deeper draft — in other words, she was more powerful. Her mast was completely made of wood (spruce) but had to support an immense triangular Bermuda-type mainsail. To take the strain, her rigging was anchored on spreaders and held in by a massive network of shrouds and jib-booms. As American and British yachts were constrained by the class regulations affecting the America's Cup, *Candida* had to be adapted several times to conform with the technical requirements, but her record of achievements featured regular victories in regattas organized in England. Sold in 1938, she was converted into a cruiser and renamed *Norlanda*. She returned to the Camper & Nicholson yard in 1946, and had two further owners before she was bought by Italian media magnate Dr. Attilio Monti, who has kept her since. In 1989, Monti decided to restore the boat to her original condition. The work, carried out in Italy at the Beconcini yard, was both massive and superb. *Candida* went back to her old name and sloop rig, fitted this time with a hollow wooden mast and a sail area that was scarcely less than she had had in her finest years. She is, of all the J-class boats to have been restored recently, the one that conforms most closely to the spirit of her original conception. Strictly speaking, she may be technically not quite so outstanding, but she has won many hearts both through her outward appearance and the pleasure she gives to the crews who have the opportunity to sail her.

*Shamrock* V was the first true J-class boat, designed by Charles E. Nicholson and launched in April 1930. Her owner, the unfortunate but gallant Sir Thomas Lipton, had the bad luck that year to run up against the most formidable American defense in the shape of four J-class yachts: *Weetamoe*,

OPPOSITE
*The Corum Sailing Team prepares to go about on board* Candida *in a stiff breeze. In the foreground, the crewmen responsible for retrieving the trimming sheets are guaranteed wet feet — at the very least!*

BELOW
*When the mainsail of a J-class starts to flap, the boom is transformed into a real battering ram. When getting under way, with other boats nearby, the helm must be moved with great care.*

## J-CLASS
## (ENDEAVOUR)

*Architect:* C. E. Nicholson
*Yard:* Camper & Nicholson
*Launched:* 1934
*Restored:* 1989
*Overall length:* 39.56 m (129 ft 9 in)
*Waterline length:* 26.88 m (88 ft 2 in)
*Maximum beam:* 6.70 m (22 ft)
*Draft:* 4.76 m (15 ft 7 in)
*Displacement:* 165 t
*Sail area:* 794 sq m (950 sq yd)

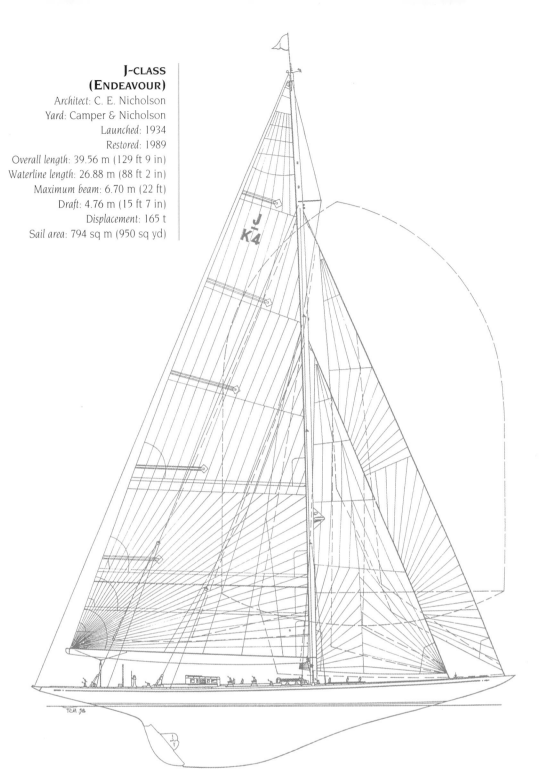

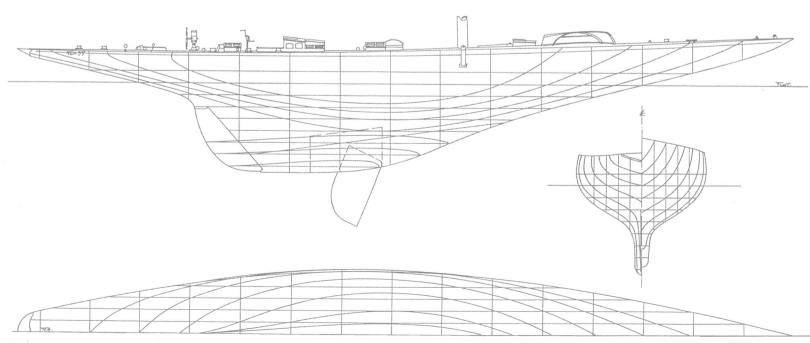

Whirlwind, Yankee, and Enterprise. The so-called Depression years were not depressing for everyone: Enterprise was the best of them and won the right to defend the America's Cup; she owed much to her twelve-sided, 49.4-meter mast, made of a light alloy and held together by 80,000 rivets. Her rig, thirty percent lighter than that of Shamrock V (the equivalent of twenty tons of lead in the keel), used a boom that was so broad they called it "Park Avenue." Her beam was such that the method of lowering the mainsail could be improved with the help of a series of small transverse rails. She was a real war machine! Shamrock V, following her defeat in the America's Cup, returned to England and was bought by T. O. M. Sopwith, who had been racing with great success in England in the summer of 1933, then by Richard Fayray, who also owned the twelve-meter class Flica. After the war, she went to the Mediterranean, where she had several Italian owners before being finally bought by the Lipton Tea Company, which presented her to the Museum of Yachting in Newport, Rhode Island, where she was restored in 1989. Now put to work as a charter boat, she sails the same waters as she did in her great days, off Newport.

Endeavour was the British challenger in 1934. Also designed by Charles Nicholson, she was owned by T. O. M. Sopwith, an aviation magnate in Britain and a helmsman with many victories to his credit, who had previously bought Shamrock V from Sir Thomas Lipton. When Lipton died, Sopwith took up the America's Cup challenge on behalf of Britain, not without success; his Endeavour came close to ending the Americans' winning run when she won the first two races in the 1934 campaign. Sherman Hoyt, the cunning American skipper of Rainbow, worked a fine tactic in the crucial third encounter and held on to win the next two races.

T. O. M. Sopwith had a new J-class for the 1937 competition: Endeavour II, which was beaten by Ranger. Only the first of Sopwith's two Endeavours has managed (quite rightly!) to hold back the years. After being restored, she enjoyed a new hour of glory, becoming the most successful J-class still sailing at the very end of the twentieth century.

Before he died, T. O. M. Sopwith was able to meet the woman who would bring new life to Endeavour. Then aged 96, he was visited at his manor house in Hampshire by an energetic slip of a woman named Elizabeth Meyer, who had firmly made up her mind to take on the crazy task of renovating Endeavour. He might have had his doubts but she had already worked on the restoration of Shamrock, as a member of the directing committee of the Museum of Yachting. After imparting some wise words of advice, he sent her to see Frank Murdoch, a talented engineer who had been his confidant at the time of the America's Cup.

And so Frank Murdoch had the pleasure of taking part in the most monumental restoration ever undertaken on a yacht. Elizabeth Meyer never lost her grip and finally realized her dream, however crazy it may have been. The hull, which had been embedded for years in a mudbank on the River Hamble near Southampton, was extracted from the mud by John and Vivienne Amos, who launched themselves, with only limited means, on the enormous work of restoring her.

OPPOSITE
Details of the deck and the interior of Endeavour, whose restoration was an enormous enterprise: the hull was recovered in a pitiful state from a mudbank; since that time, she has become one of the most beautiful boats in the world.

ABOVE
Endeavour sailing close-hauled: she is a formidable machine for tacking close to the wind.

PAGES 134–5
Candida sailing close-hauled in a breeze. The waves can do one of two things: smash against the boat or pass on by.

RIGHT
On the starting line,
it is better not to find
yourself to leeward
of a J-class, or you
can be sure of getting
no wind for several
minutes.

Elizabeth Meyer bought the boat, and then supplied the necessary funds to complete the work. In 1936, when she was again able to float, *Endeavour* was towed to the Royal Huismann yard in the Netherlands, one of the best shipyards in the world. In spring 1989 she emerged, and once more became the most formidable racing machine of her day. Every time a race could be arranged, *Endeavour* dominated her old rivals, soundly defeating *Shamrock* at Newport, New York, and Annapolis in 1989 and 1990, and *Astra* and *Candida* at the Nioulargue. Only *Velsheda*, which had been restored in 1989 and equipped with a carbon-fiber mast, was able to give her a really hard time.

The J-class *Velsheda* belonged to W. L. Stephenson, the chairman of the Woolworth company in England. His boat took her name from a combination of his daughters' first names: Velma, Sheila, and Daphne. She was built in 1933 — also at Camper & Nicholson — and restored several times. In 1988 she was to be seen sailing at Douarnenez, then during the classic season in the Mediterranean, where she made a great impression by virtue of her size, although she was not as well maintained, or in such a good state of repair, as her peers. In 1997 she was finally given her present-day appearance by Southampton Yacht Services. The side access plates disappeared, the hull was painted navy blue, her deck was remade in teak. The carbon-fiber mast was the biggest ever made up to the time of her relaunch. Her mainsail, made of Vectran, was half the weight of the original, and the sails were worked by a battery of hydraulic winches. Twenty tons were removed from the keel but some of the weight loss was made up again by a mass of new equipment such as motors, generators, various refrigeration systems, and even washing machines. Although she has largely lost her authenticity, *Velsheda* remains a very impressive yet elegant boat that ranks among the elite of the superyachts. She is also privileged to carry on her mainsail the famous "J" mark — an exclusive distinction reserved for the aristocracy of racing.

ABOVE
Everything aboard a
J-class is enormous.

TOP
To clear a fouled
sheet, a crewman
has to be hoisted in
the air with the help
of a halyard.

## ALTAÏR
## Setting standards
## for all

Despite her recent record of carrying off all the trophies at traditional yacht rallies, Altaïr is not, and never has been, a racing boat. From the very beginning, Altaïr was commissioned, designed and built as a cruising yacht. It is just that the restoration of this gaff-rigged schooner, carried out in 1987 by Southampton Yacht Services in England, was so exemplary, and the way she has been handled since her rebirth has always been so perfect, that she gathers victories and arouses admiration with ease, to the point where she has become, and will remain, the ultimate standard-setter for all classic yachts.

Altaïr is to some extent the boat that started it all. As one of those yachts that have inspired wealthy people not only to want to possess a boat of this kind, but also to restore it in the spirit of a wonderful tradition, she has launched careers for many others. When you see Altaïr sail by, you too want to sail, and to do it well. She tempts you to get on a boat and cast off. You want to be there, hoisting the sails. This is why Altaïr is such an exemplary boat — one of the founders of the renaissance in classic yachts.

A few years ago, at the Nioulargue, Altaïr was closely followed by one of the press boats, packed as ever with photographers and specialist journalists — the kind of people who are always around the most beautiful boats on the planet, crossing the world in the course of the year from Newport to Auckland, from the America's Cup to the Whitbread. Altaïr was sailing close-hauled up the Gulf of Saint-Tropez against a small but impressive mistral. After a few minutes of cameras clicking with unbelievable density, the noise gradually abated and then, amazingly, the silence became total. All the best photographers and journalists of the day just looked on, so taken were they by the beauty of what lay before them. They had suddenly stopped work, taking time out to watch Altaïr sail. Her bow cut finely through the lapping waves, her natural-colored sails — a great novelty at that time — caught as much wind as they could and channeled it aft. The crew, impeccably dressed in white uniforms, were quietly ranged along the bulwark to windward. There was no sound aboard, no halyard flapping — only the rustling of the wind in the sails and the moist whisper of the bow wave. Maneuvers were made in a flash, without anyone speaking, with no voice raised above the others. The helmsman, deep in concentration, followed the breeze by luffing a few degrees as the wind increased the boat's heel. It was a breathtakingly beautiful sight.

OPPOSITE AND ABOVE
*This is Altaïr, so smooth and elegant, so well turned out — one of the first boats to be restored to her full magnificence. The Fife-designed schooner shows no sign of age, and makes people dream every time she sails. Could she be the perfect boat?*

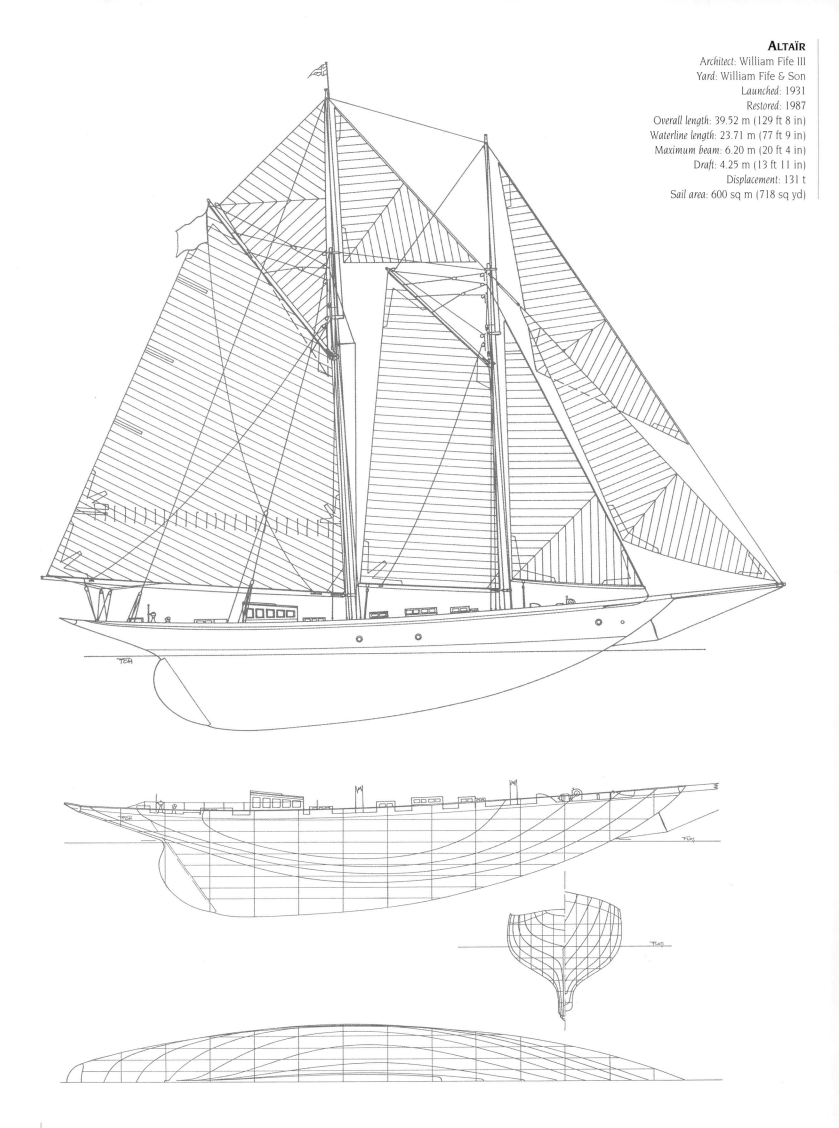

**ALTAÏR**

*Architect:* William Fife III
*Yard:* William Fife & Son
*Launched:* 1931
*Restored:* 1987
*Overall length:* 39.52 m (129 ft 8 in)
*Waterline length:* 23.71 m (77 ft 9 in)
*Maximum beam:* 6.20 m (20 ft 4 in)
*Draft:* 4.25 m (13 ft 11 in)
*Displacement:* 131 t
*Sail area:* 600 sq m (718 sq yd)

If proof were needed of her pedigree, Altaïr is, moreover, a Fife design built at the Fife yard in Fairlie, Scotland, near the estuary of the River Clyde. From this magical place, of which nothing now remains, came some of the most beautiful boats in the world, in a real class of their own. William Fife III was already seventy-five years old when he designed Altaïr for Capt. Guy H. MacCaw, who wanted a reliable cruiser to sail to the Southern Seas. Launched in 1931, in his hands the boat never went beyond the waters off Gascony in southwest France. With her next proprietor, Walter Runciman, she again stayed close to the British coast. Runciman apparently prided himself on taking part in a few regattas at Cowes. After one more owner, Sir William Verdon-Smith, and a war in which she was forced to do patrol duty, Altaïr was at last able to enjoy a taste of the South when she was bought by a Portuguese owner. He kept her for two years and in 1950 sold her to a Spaniard from Barcelona named Miguel San Mora, who made her his personal yacht for thirty-four years.

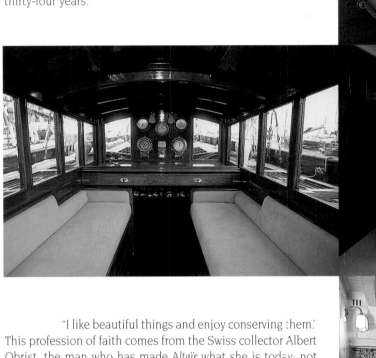

"I like beautiful things and enjoy conserving them." This profession of faith comes from the Swiss collector Albert Obrist, the man who has made Altaïr what she is today: not only the reference point for all classic yachts but also the first to have been restored. The work was carried out with uncompromising attention to authenticity. The task was considerable, but everything that could be retained from the original boat was kept. The keel had to be modified to resolve problems affecting her trim, but the lead used at Fairlie was recast so that the original Altaïr should live on with everything in keeping. If a rib was damaged, the sound part was kept and a new section with a chamfered edge was just glued on. Part of the metal structure of the interior had to be changed, together with some of the surrounding woodwork, which was damaged; the pine deck was replaced by one of teak, and the running rigging, delivered by Harry Spencer, was reminiscent of the most ancient of manual technologies. The sails, although made of Tergal, created a precedent as they had been dyed to produce the natural look of period cotton. "Home comforts" such as a desalinator, a freezer, and a washing machine were added, but were hidden behind bulkheads, and the original water tanks were in sufficiently good condition to be kept. Although there are some winches on the deck, they have been fitted with bronze heads so that they integrate perfectly with the rest of the gear.

ABOVE
View of the
doghouse; the period
instruments; the
central saloon; the aft
cabin.

PAGES 142–3
As the crew hangs
over the sea and
the wind is aft,
Altaïr's sails open
out like flowers.

RIGHT
*When the sea is rough and the wind steady, then the only thing that flies is the spray. This calls for real sailing.*

Over the seasons there has emerged a certain quality, not immediately noticeable, but which might be called the manners of a boat. It shows itself in small details — tiny things which mark out certain sailboats as closer than others to the great traditions of yachting. They have standards or rules which ensure, for example, that even if the boat were to be caught by surprise at the back of a Greek harbor in November, the brass would still be impeccable and the sails would be tidily stowed; a flag would be flying on the correct halyard, the sails would be in their proper place whatever the circumstances, and the crew would be as quiet and solicitous as ever. When boats arrive together, and others have long since switched on their engines, this boat will be sailing, and will suddenly make a quick and successful maneuver, whatever the conditions, achieving this without anyone raising their voice. *Altaïr* is just such a boat, where the pleasure of sailing, and doing it properly, comes before all other considerations. It is easy to be flashy or impeccably turned out for a week at the Nioulargue. To keep it up for several seasons running, despite changes of crew and even of owner, is a quite different matter. This requires a deeper sense of maritime manners, a true love of yachts and sailing for pleasure. Some boats inspire their people with these feelings more than others. *Altaïr* is one of them.

ABOVE
*Handling this canvas
is a pleasure, sailing
in this boat is an
honor, watching her
sail a real delight.*

# OISEAU DE FEU
## One for the Atlantic

Oiseau de feu is an example of tit for tat. In this case the pretty monohull, called *Firebird* X when she was launched in England in 1936, was one of the defensive weapons created by English yachtsmen to combat the growing appetite of American racers, especially those who had come over and won the Fastnet two years running with a terribly annoying boat named *Dorade*. She was one of the boats designed by Charles Nicholson, then at the height of his glory, to counter the rather too effective imagination of the exceptional young New Yorker Olin Stephens, creator of *Dorade*. At this time the yachting world was making the most of the tremendous golden age of the 1930s to discover ocean racing in boats made to sail far from the English coast, whatever the weather. As well as meeting these criteria, *Oiseau de feu* was also a yacht which offered enough comforts to serve as a pleasant cruiser. From the day she began she was two boats in one.

She came into being at the Camper & Nicholson yard in Southampton, England, after the firm's chief had received a commission for a boat capable of winning the inshore and, in particular, the offshore regattas of the British racing season. These events were known as the Admiral's Cup, the Fastnet, Falmouth to the Azores, and the Channel Race. The owner who wished to take on such a program was none other than the commodore of the Royal Ocean Racing Club. He was named Ralph Hawks and he was one of a line of skippers who were noted old sea dogs, never afraid to brave bad weather while they were racing. The English yachtsmen's other defensive weapons were launched at about the same time under the names of *Foxhound*, *Bloodhound*, and *Stiarna* — a virtual armada created entirely by Charles Nicholson. For *Firebird* X he conceived, in the Olin Stephens tradition, a deep, narrow boat inspired by the efficiency of international class designs.

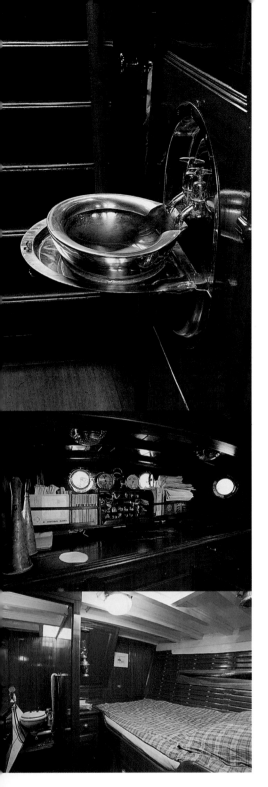

## OISEAU DE FEU

Architect: C. E. Nicholson
Yard: Camper & Nicholson
Launched: 1936
Restored: 1991
Overall length: 19.35 m (63 ft 6 in)
Waterline length: 14.63 m (48 ft)
Maximum beam: 3.66 m (12 ft)
Draft: 2.51 m (8 ft 3 in)
Displacement: 40 t
Sail area: 210 sq m (251 sq yd)

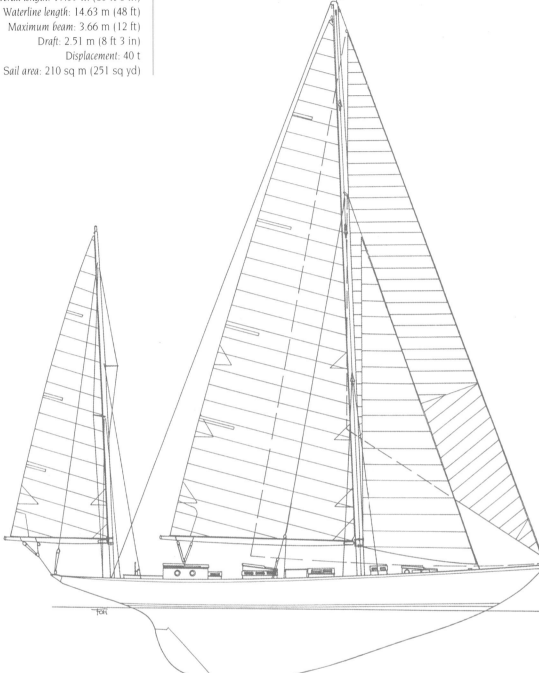

*ABOVE*
*There is a small retractable wash basin at the foot of the companionway; the chart table located forward of the doghouse; view of the forward cabin with a head.*

*RIGHT*
*A classic decorative style for the saloon, enhanced by a model of a clinker-built sailing dinghy.*

Equipped with a single mast and a Bermuda-type mainsail, her rigging was fixed to a long bowsprit forward, athwartships on shrouds with spreaders, and aft to a fishtail backstay. Her very long boom allowed her to carry an impressive mainsail, while forward her sails were divided variously into yankees, staysails and jibs.

Once she was launched, *Firebird* X carried out her mission with honor, being highly placed in races up to World War II, then passing to another owner, Mr. Hugh M. Crankshaw, at the close of hostilities. He gave her a yawl rig, though this in no way prevented her from racing until the beginning of the 1950s in the hands of another skipper, a certain Mr. Green.

Great changes were made to *Firebird* in 1963, when she crossed the English Channel and passed under the French flag. This new epoch began with Pierre Cointreau, who renamed her *Flame* II and sailed her for seven years exclusively as a cruiser. A number of great French sailors, including some of the most famous, have emotional memories of this boat. She was so large and beautiful that in the 1950s she looked like a giant in the little Breton harbor of La Trinité-sur-Mer. Every local boy dreamed of being able to go aboard this extraordinary and already legendary sailboat, even if it was only to have an opportunity to coil the lines or sweep the deck.

TOP RIGHT
*Wheel detail showing the boat's name hand-engraved in the stainless steel band.*

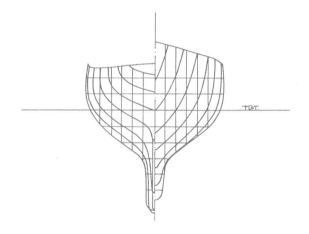

The next two owners were French too. The politician Henri Rey sailed her mainly in the Mediterranean for three years, during which time the boat was known as *Vindilis* II, before he yielded ownership, in 1976, to Michel Perroud, a knowledgeable racer hailing from La Rochelle. He restored the original name of the Nicholson-designed boat, albeit translated into French, calling her *Oiseau de feu*. From then on he sailed her intensively, putting together a string of all-out races and in the course of these discovering the power of those large foresails from another age, known as Genoa jibs. He also undertook long cruises to Ireland, Spain, and the Azores. The winter of 1983 was marked by a series of heavy storms. Isolated at her moorings in the river below Auray, *Oiseau de feu* broke her cable and was ripped open on an oyster bed. Never mind: she was refloated, repaired, her interior was refitted, and she set off as good as ever on four further years of sailing in the Mediterranean and the Atlantic.

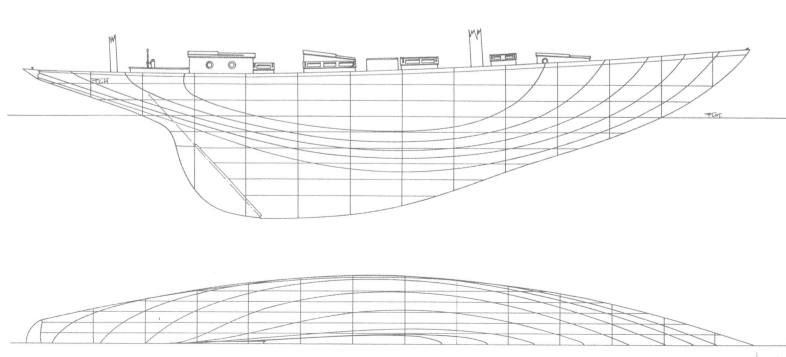

PAGES 152–3
Oiseau de feu is a
traditional yacht
decorated with a fine
collection of maritime
objects, as revealed by
this cabinet located in
the saloon.

RIGHT
A pile of the bronze
hanks which allow
the foresails to slide
along the stays.

In 1989 her present owner, Pierre Lembo, fell madly for her timeless thoroughbred silhouette. It was clear to him that she would have to undergo a wide-ranging refit if she were to sail to her full potential. This mission was entrusted to the architect Guy Ribadeau-Dumas and the Raymond Labbé yard at Saint-Malo. Unfortunately, as sometimes happens in this type of situation, some unpleasant surprises came to light on the way, notably the bad condition of the composite hull: the metal parts were eaten up with rust and had even caused some of the surrounding timbers to rot. The beautiful *Oiseau de feu* had to be plucked to the bone and then largely rebuilt. During this process, Guy Ribadeau-Dumas designed a more powerful rigging to help her sail better in light conditions, and with the wind aft of the beam thanks to the addition of a 300-square-meter spinnaker made by Victor Tonerre. For her new destiny as a family cruiser she also received some electric winches to make her easier to maneuver with a small crew. As for the interior arrangements, they were patiently reconstructed from original plans discovered in the Museum of London, which gave her back all her former sparkle. In the style of what they do best in Britain, *Oiseau de feu*, which can today be considered a French boat, has had the good fortune to be born again, thanks to the determination of her owners to make her restoration authentic. Today she races and cruises with equal flair. She owes much to the skilled knowledge of a team of craftsmen who love their work, and also to those wooden boats that give us so much to dream about.

BELOW
*Detail of the rack where halyards can be clipped when not in use; and the compass housing.*

BOTTOM
Oiseau de feu *going about in a good breeze in the days when she was rigged as a yawl.*

# Brest–Douarnenez

---

Brittany has always been the most maritime region of France, and it is not surprising that the people there, as much from cultural tradition as economic necessity, have a natural passion for boats.

Nor is it surprising that it should be in Douarnenez, facing the ocean from the very edge of Europe, that the enormous groundswell should have started which pushed the good people of France into finally taking an interest in their maritime heritage. It was in Douarnenez that the magazine of maritime history and ethnology *Le Chasse-marée* was founded and still runs today. And it was here that people started to restore old sailing boats. The French Coastal Boats movement also began in Douarnenez, helping to find, save, and restore dozens of boats which had almost vanished and which are witnesses to their maritime past. And it was also in Douarnenez that they established the Harbor Museum, aimed at bringing before the public these vintage boats that have been so splendidly reconstructed.

It has to be admitted that, with the notable exception of *Pen Duick*, most of the architects, yards, and owners responsible for the rebirth of these beautiful classic yachts are British or Italian. It is a question of tradition, no doubt — a question of means, too, but above all a question of culture. Boats and the sea do not have the same place in French society, particularly in the wealthiest circles, as they do in Great Britain and Italy. If at the end of the eighteenth century French naval architects such as Gustave Caillebotte or Godinet were very well known, they mostly designed sailboats of modest proportions, of which almost nothing remains today.

## Under the aegis of *Le Chasse-marée*

On the other hand, the vintage working boats in the process of being restored were sufficiently numerous and geographically scattered for the French Coastal Boats competition, launched by *Le Chasse-marée*, to be very successful. The displays of old rigs, which had begun at Pors-Beac'h in 1982, came to the fore in 1989 with the first giant rally of vintage boats, staged in Rouen as part of the bicentenary celebrations of the French Revolution. These events continued at Douarnenez every other year, notably at Brest in 1992 and 1996, and were so successful that they became known to the rest of French society. How could it be otherwise, given the dozens of small municipal authorities distributed along the whole coastline, each

*ABOVE AND BELOW LEFT*
*The rallies at Brest and Douarnenez attract more big sailing boats and working craft than yachts built for pleasure, but are tremendously successful with the public.*

*OPPOSITE*
*The bow wave of a Breton cutter.*

*ABOVE*
*Brest harbor besieged by vintage rigs: from marine painters to sea craftsmen, the displays at Brest and Douarnenez are both cultural and maritime occasions.*

*OPPOSITE*
*A bucket of sea water and a brush — two indispensable tools on board every wooden boat.*

*PAGES 160–61*
*"One day I'll go to sea ..."*

invest in the restoration of a traditional boat? How could it not have reached this stage when thousands of people hurry to the quayside at Brest to look at the thousand and one vessels newly arisen from the past, of all shapes and sizes, all origins and nationalities, all mixed up together?

Brest and Douarnenez are in it together. The boats at these rallies are for the most part smaller and less luxurious than those appearing in the Mediterranean rallies. Originally they were working boats rather than yachts built for pleasure, but these meetings have taken on such an importance, tapping into the minds of so many people, and forming such a colossal collective fair, that many vintage sailing boats, built for pleasure, come and join in these great maritime festivals.

## A formidable brew

It's not a question here of classy private gatherings, but of a tremendous burst of collective and cultural enthusiasm, rich and varied beyond belief. At Brest, in four days of celebrations and almost uninterrupted meetings, you can see every imaginable type of boat on the water: Thames barges, lighters, little fishing cutters, three-masters, clippers, corsair boats, international class boats, tiny sailing prams, canoes, pilot boats, and others. On land, too, the choice is no less impressive. You certainly have to do some walking, and sometimes you feel overwhelmed by the endlessly moving crowd, but the discoveries you make are as picturesque as they are unexpected and varied: artisans who have revived the ancient traditions of the sea, folklore groups, organizations trying to restore a whole boat during the course of the festival, grandmothers weaving skeins of cotton. On the water, by the estuary of the Sambre, old coquillers are fishing under sail as a superb schooner arrives from America. *Pen Duick* is at the fête, of course, and the two last training ships, *Étoile* and *Belle Poule*. *Belem* is not far away, and you can even see the pointed shapes of Mediterranean feluccas, junks, Dutch barges with their lee-boards in the shape of a butterfly's wing, and boats that have come from the Far East. The most striking moment is without question the enormous communal voyage which takes a large part of the fleet from Brest to Douarnenez to continue the party, and even beyond to the great ocean which opens up between the island ramparts of Sein and Ouessant. The sea is a party, and Brest and Douarnenez are its harbors.

## Thendara
# The end of an era,
# the beginning of a reign

It is impossible to miss *Thendara* at today's rallies of classic yachts. Not only is she one of the largest and fastest, she is also one of the few to be rigged as a gaff-rigged ketch. Accordingly, each of her two masts supports a trapezoid sail surmounted by a jackyard topsail, giving her a silhouette that is at once imposing and very characteristic. This original rig was one of *Thendara*'s special features when she was launched in April 1937 at the yard of Alexander Stephens & Sons, situated at Linthouse, a Scottish village on the Clyde estuary. The first Bermuda rigs, with their triangular mainsails, had already appeared on European racing yachts several seasons before, and had begun irreversibly to assert their superiority over gaff-rigged boats. This great turnabout did not greatly worry Arthur Young, the Scottish yachtsman who gave the commission for *Thendara* to his compatriot, the architect Alfred Mylne. Mylne's output is certainly admirable even if his present reputation is not as high as Fife's. He designed boats for nearly fifty years, and they were often highly placed in races. He worked beside George L. Watson on the modifications made to *Britannia*, the famous British royal yacht which raced for almost forty years before being scuttled on the death of George V.

*Thendara* certainly marked the end of an era for the yard of Alexander Stephens & Sons, which from then on devoted itself to making vessels for the Royal Navy — an activity that soon became essential during World War II. *Thendara* was requisitioned at the time and transformed into a training ship for conscripts, which did not do her general condition much good. Returned to her owner once peace was signed, she had to go back to the yard to be fitted with a bow and bulwarks worthy of her. She then resumed her peacetime career as an ocean cruiser until the day, in 1950, when Sir Arthur Young died on board while she was moored off Bénodet in Brittany.

OPPOSITE
*Aboard* Thendara,
*as on most classic
yachts, the crews
working the foresails
have their work cut
out. The general
effectiveness of the sail
plan depends on
getting a good flow of
wind between the
different sails.*

ABOVE
Thendara *doesn't
like big waves,
and they don't
like her either.*

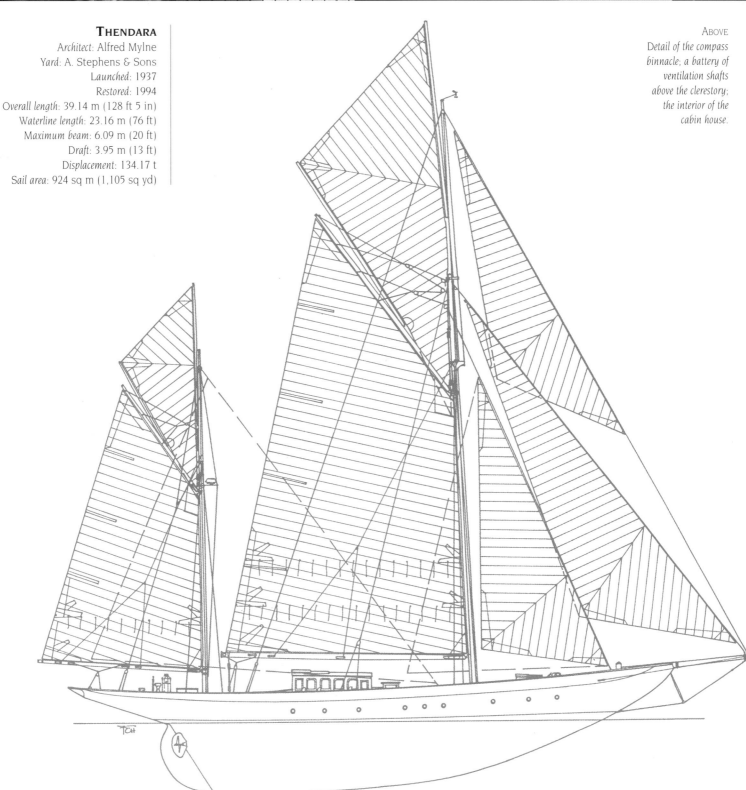

### THENDARA

Architect: Alfred Mylne
Yard: A. Stephens & Sons
Launched: 1937
Restored: 1994
Overall length: 39.14 m (128 ft 5 in)
Waterline length: 23.16 m (76 ft)
Maximum beam: 6.09 m (20 ft)
Draft: 3.95 m (13 ft)
Displacement: 134.17 t
Sail area: 924 sq m (1,105 sq yd)

ABOVE
Detail of the compass
binnacle; a battery of
ventilation shafts
above the clerestory;
the interior of the
cabin house.

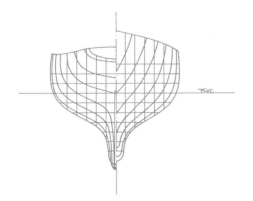

*Thendara* also marks the temporary end of an era in the sense that racing boats built after the war were often much smaller in size. Fitted with a new Bermuda rig, the great ketch went off to Greece, a destination for all yacht cruises, before she was bought by the Italian owner who carried out her first restoration from 1986 to 1988 at La Spezia. This was not brought to completion, however, and *Thendara* had to wait until 1994 before going to the yard of Southampton Yacht Services in the south of England, where she underwent the major restoration that marked the beginning of her new life.

To look at *Thendara* today, you would think she had been rebuilt exactly as she was at birth — and it is true that her external appearance and her interior arrangements are those of a classic yacht, from the base of her keel to the top of her mast. However, behind her bulkheads and planking the luxurious ketch conceals the most modern equipment, making her a unique cruiser offering the highest degree of comfort. On deck, for example, the galvanized steel hoisting gear is original but the winch for the mainsail halyard has been fitted with an electric servo-control. This means that a small crew, of the kind you often get on cruises and in convoys, can safely carry out the standard maneuver of raising the mainsail while leaving a harbor or moorings. It is also good for safety when the wind gets up and they have to

reduce sail and take in reefs. Another example: the cabins have been restored with extreme attention to detail, even as far as faithfully replacing hinges to the original design; yet these very same cabins are equipped with air-conditioning to supplement the natural ventilation, which, as on board all vintage yachts, is far from adequate. This makes a big difference when it comes to sailing in the Mediterranean in summer. It is easy to imagine how sweet life must be on such a yacht when, on a fine summer's evening, the time comes to sit round the outside table, which is put up forward of the coach. The galley, located forward near the crew's quarters, has all the necessary equipment worthy of such a cruiser. Later you can take a final drink in the deckhouse or go and leaf through a good book below, on the sofa in the saloon. The general decorations marry furniture in Honduran mahogany with other surfaces painted an agreeable cream color, as is the fashion aboard vintage yachts.

TOP
*The main saloon aboard* Thendara *is divided into two parts, with the dining table to starboard and the sofa to port. Like other boats intended for extensive use as cruisers,* Thendara *is today equipped with an air-conditioning system.*

165

PAGES 166–7
Thendara *close-hauled off Saint-Tropez. There is a steady breeze and the small jackyard topsail has been rigged above the mainsail.*

RIGHT
Thendara *close-hauled with all sails set. Her two gaff-rigged sails give her a silhouette that everyone recognizes.*

For racing, the crew can easily be expanded to twenty members, as *Thendara* is a very big boat measuring nearly forty meters (130 feet) overall and displacing more than 130 tons. You need a lot of elbow power to manipulate the twelve sails in her wardrobe, and the various bronze-headed winches that are available on the deck are of scant help: most maneuvers have to be carried out by hand which demands strength, experience, and organization. No less than two miles of line are required to raise or control all her sails, and this is hauled in, turned round, or hoisted through more than 150 blocks (most of which bear an individual plaque bearing the crest of the boat).

In a few seasons, *Thendara* has become one of the most successful sailboats on the classic yacht circuit. As the miles have added up, her crew has found out about her, and they now bring her to every event with all drums beating. In this way, the luff of the foresails has been brought progressively closer to the wind when she sails close-hauled, and when she is running with the wind she can sail directly in the direction of the wind more efficiently, rather than having to make long tacks. The crew have also demonstrated a certain superiority in their technique for rounding buoys.

Against *Altaïr* and *Mariette*, her two main rivals, *Thendara* regularly wins the upper hand. She still tends to hold back when she has to power through a rough sea, as her more extended lines and smaller displacement make her pitch impressively. Jacques Louvel, the boat's present skipper, has a distinctly uncomfortable memory of 1,500 miles of close-hauled sailing on the great New York–Southampton race for classic boats in 1997. But that is the fate of all sailing boats everywhere: the wind and the sea are not always what we might have wished for.

ABOVE
A *race to the finish at the Voiles d'Antibes between* Thendara *(who crosses the line first) and* Shenandoah — *a very beautiful sight.*

# 12-m class

12-M CLASS

1950 | The queens of America

The international classification system has always been heavily criticized, even before it came into existence, during its finest years and even today. The boats it created were thought too heavy, too slow, while the system itself did not stimulate enough technical innovation, and was too narrow for the architects' imaginations. Maybe — but we could answer the detractors by saying that no system of classification is perfect, that few others have brought so many yachts into being over such a long period, and that the system has allowed thousands of yachtsmen to satisfy their desires and to achieve memorable feats, up to and including the champions of the America's Cup who made twelve-meter class yachts their warhorses for almost thirty years.

The last "Cup" to be decided by these famous "twelves" was one of the finest of all. It took place in 1983 off Newport, Rhode Island, where John Bertrand and the keel fins of *Australia* II succeeded in ending 132 years of American domination of the Cup. The sight of these heavy boats — powerful, physically exhausting for their crews, equipped with a monstrously large sail area — engaged in homeric battles in the strong Atlantic winds, will remain in the memories of those who lived through those unforgettable moments. Like all heavy boats, the twelve-meters are spectacular because they displace more water and reduce the waves to an explosion of spray. Their huge collection of sails, their booms skimming the deck, their low freeboard, the lack of guard rails, and their tiny cockpits where the crew are thrown against each other like a rugby scrum, are just some of the features which add a very spectacular dimension to the classical elegance of the twelve-meter class boats.

ABOVE
Adjusting the Genoa
jibs aboard Flica II,
one of the oldest
"twelves" still sailing
now. She was designed
by William Fife III.

OPPOSITE
Immortalized in the
America's Cup, the
twelve-meter class boats
often come in pairs.
Here French Kiss
(red spinnaker) races
against the English
White Crusader off
Fremantle, Western
Australia.

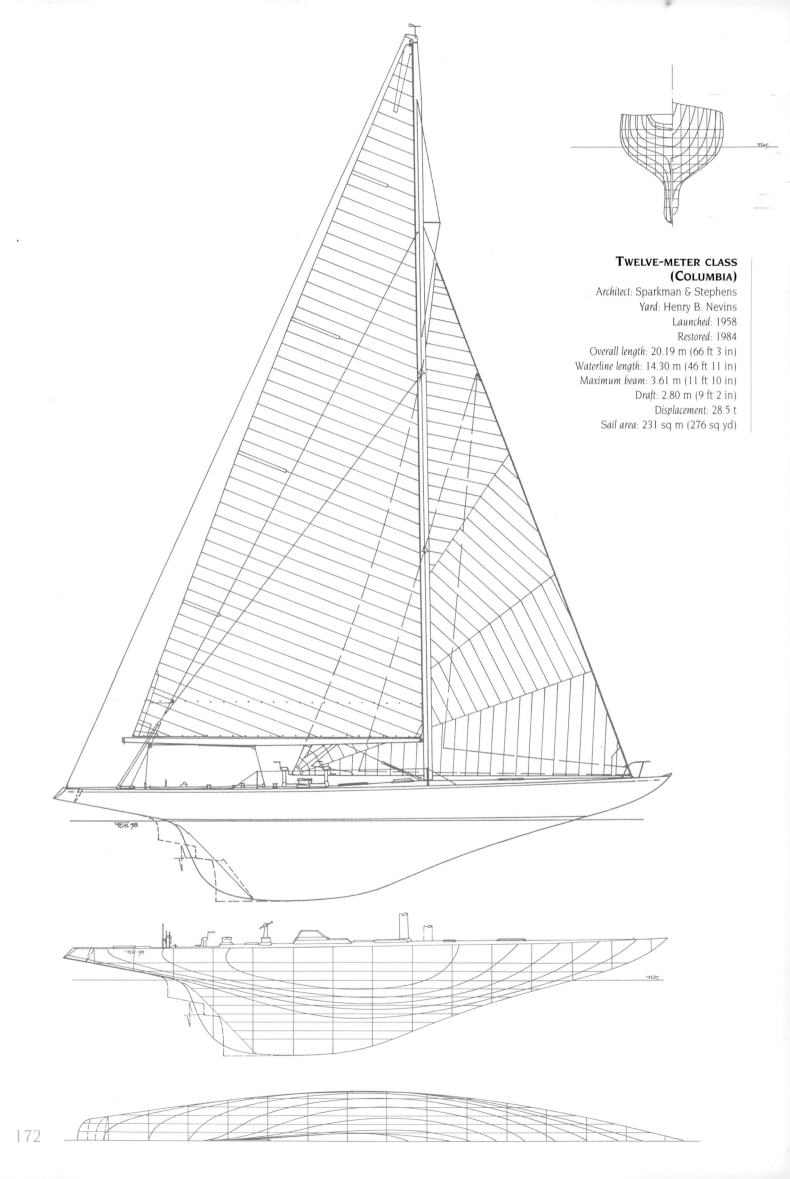

**TWELVE-METER CLASS
(COLUMBIA)**
*Architect:* Sparkman & Stephens
*Yard:* Henry B. Nevins
*Launched:* 1958
*Restored:* 1984
*Overall length:* 20.19 m (66 ft 3 in)
*Waterline length:* 14.30 m (46 ft 11 in)
*Maximum beam:* 3.61 m (11 ft 10 in)
*Draft:* 2.80 m (9 ft 2 in)
*Displacement:* 28.5 t
*Sail area:* 231 sq m (276 sq yd)

Like all the international class boats, the first twelve-meters were powered by gaff rigs, but few of these have been restored or are sailing today with their original rig, except for *Cintra*, a Fife design that sails little but made a noted appearance in 1991 during the classic yachts season in the Mediterranean.

Very soon the "twelves" were equipped with Bermuda rigs and fitted with everything that technology could possibly give them within the very strict constraints of the class: winches, and aluminum masts and hulls. The first computers were installed on the "twelves," as well as the first Dacron sails and the first sails made of Mylar/Kevlar, and the first keels with fins. While they remain a famous and much-disparaged class, one of the articles compels adherence to Lloyd's specifications, thus making the twelve-meters virtually indestructible, which is the reason that most of them are still sailing today.

So it has been with *Flica* II, one of the veterans of the class designed by Laurent Giles and built at the Fife yard in Fairlie in 1929. Already, even then, *Flica* was lucky enough to be given a keel designed after tests on five different models at the testing tank of the Stevens Institute in New Jersey. She had already won several races when she was joined by other twelve-meter boats that can still be seen sailing today. First, in 1937, came *Trivia*, presently based in Monaco, and then *Vim*, Harold Vanderbilt's twelve-meter which carried all before her in the 1939 season, and finally *Tomahawk*, which belonged to T. O. M. Sopwith and had been designed by Charles Nicholson. She was one of the best British racing yachts of the pre-war period. All these boats were made of wood and equipped with very basic interior arrangements.

The British twelve-meter boats designed in the 1950s were entrusted with a mission of a quite different caliber: that of bringing back the America's Cup!

The era of the enormous J-class boats came to end with World War II, and the yachting authorities were in effect forced to rely on a smaller type of boat than the J-class, though just as competitive and above all capable of finding owners at a time of economic uncertainty.

LEFT
*Cintra, one of the rare twelve-meter boats with a gaff rig still surviving today.*

RIGHT
*Details of the helm and the interior arrangements aboard Nyala.*

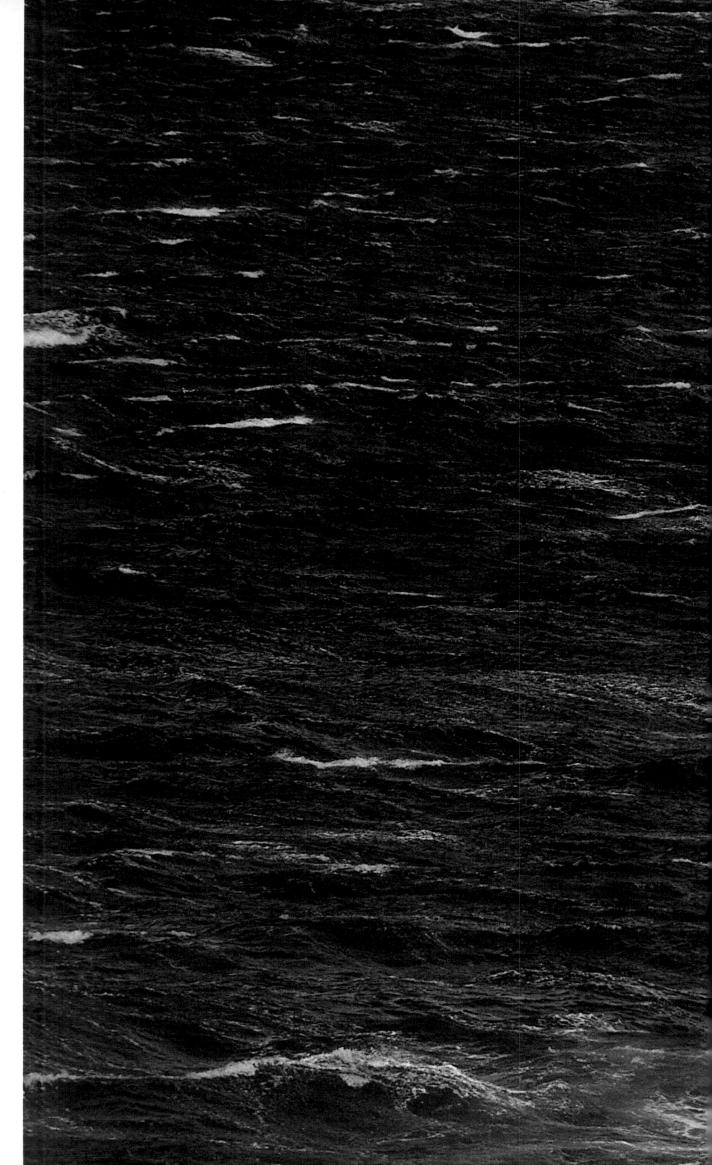

PAGES 174–5
A regatta on the
waters off Fremantle
— one of the very
rare occasions when
multiple-entry races
have taken place in
the strong breezes off
Western Australia. To
see these boats on the
open sea is a real
photographer's
dream.

RIGHT
The twelve-meter
Sovereign tries to
survive a blast from
the mistral in the
Mediterranean.
Like all international
class boats, the
"twelves" are not
really adapted to
sailing in a wind
— the crews
would agree!

RIGHT
Coming about in a
twelve-meter class
yacht is an art which
demands a good
touch and a certain
patience. It takes
quite a while to
recover the speed
lost after turning
head to wind.

The first "twelve" to be built after the war was *Columbia*, which is also still sailing today. She won the 1958 version of the Cup, thanks to the speed which the pencil of Olin Stephens had given her since birth.

After this, the New York "wizard" produced a ceaseless flow of ever more competitive boats, finally reaching the peak of his glory with *Courageous*, the first twelve-meter class made of aluminum. *Courageous* succeeded in defending the America's Cup twice running, on one occasion in the hands of the future media magnate Ted Turner. He served again as a pacemaker in 1983 before trying his luck again in 1987 — though without great hopes — at Fremantle, after the Australians had carried off the famous "Auld Mug." Although these boats do not provoke technological innovation, the twelve-meter class was at the heart of a tremendous revolution in sailing when the famous fin keel of *Australia* II made its appearance.

In 1983, the Australian millionaire Alan Bond challenged the America's Cup for the second time. At that period, the trophy was slumbering peacefully in the confines of the New York Yacht Club, such was the superiority of the American racers and their favorite architect, Olin Stephens. But a group of rather different men — Alan Bond the financier, Ben Lexcen the shrewd architect, Peter Van Ossanen the Dutch expert in hydrodynamics, and John Bertrand the implacable skipper — took the crazy gamble of fitting the keel of *Australia* II with large lateral fins. The concept had been tested before on a number of cruisers, but never in competition and even less so in the framework of the America's Cup. Easier to handle, with better acceleration, sailing better both close to the wind and with the wind aft of the beam, *Australia* II was the shock of the 1983 Cup, exciting even more comment because the famous keel was invariably kept under wraps at all times. Dennis Conner, who in *Liberty*

had only a very classical boat, would have needed all his knowledge to match the suspense. The result, which took the whole world by surprise, was greeted with unprecedented public excitement: a score of four wins to three, with *Australia* II only managing to pass *Liberty* on the penultimate tack of the final round. When the boat from Down Under went irretrievably past, Dennis Conner uttered these still famous words that apply to all racing boats: "If one of you has an idea now is the time to say it." But the "idea" was something he should have thought of before the race. It was such a good idea that most cruisers are fitted with it today.

TOP
*The care bestowed
on classic yachts
extends even as far
the way the mooring
lines are coiled.*

ABOVE
*Nyala and Vim side by side: the
helmsmen use the tremendous
inertia of the twelve-meter boats to
coast up closer to the wind and
blanket their nearest opponents.*

Agneta

## AGNETA
## The magic of wood

1948

On the classic yacht circuit, *Agneta* is a remarkable and much-admired boat. To look at, she seems younger, much fresher. The elegance of her lines earns her a place among the high-fliers of sailing — boats such as *Avel*, *Pen Duick*, or *Tuiga*. *Agneta* is above all a hymn to wooden construction, illustrating the tremendous richness of this material.

As though to emphasize her difference in age, appearance and performance, *Agneta* is rigged as a Bermuda-rigged yawl, characterized by two masts of unequal length (the mizzen being clearly smaller and stepped aft of the steering gear) carrying triangular sails. These are very original looking with their deep-brown color and are recognized everywhere. When the sun sets over the horizon, they vibrate with really beautiful orangy reflections.

The most notable of *Agneta*'s characteristics is, of course, her hull made of varnished mahogany. It is easy to imagine what a headache the daily maintenance of this *objet d'art* must be, and it is always surprising to find her in an impeccable condition which never varies, season after season. To obtain a finish of such quality, the upper part of the hull (the part which is out of the water) must be completely sanded down and revarnished at least once a year. "Not just once but twice a year!" Antonio, the present skipper, confirms, raising his eyes to the heavens. "There is no varnish these days which will last for a full year. After six months, small imperfections start to appear here and there, and we have to deal with them before they get any bigger. If we waited a whole year, it would be an impossible task." Almost as frequently, too, the superstructures, the masts and the interior arrangements, which are made entirely of wood, have to be finely sanded down and then given two coats of the magic varnish. It is a really Herculean task.

OPPOSITE
*It's impossible not to recognize the wine-dark sails of Agneta, or to ignore the hull of this jewel of a boat, which has to be revarnished at least twice a year.*

## AGNETA

Architect: Knud H. Reimers
Yard: Plyms
Launched: 1948
Overall length: 25.02 m (82 ft 1 in)
Waterline length: 18.13 m (59 ft 6 in)
Maximum beam: 4.42 m (14 ft 6 in)
Draft: 3 m (3 ft 3 in)
Displacement: 36 t
Sail area: 220 sq m (263 sq yd)

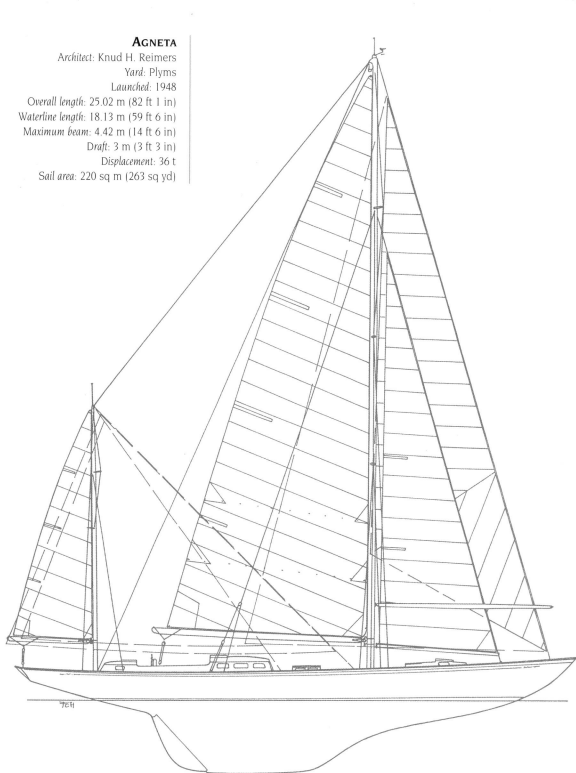

*Agneta* became famous thanks to the man who was her loving owner for almost twenty years, the Italian industrialist Gianni Agnelli, and also thanks to her record of achievements: she sails fast, is sailed hard in regattas and wins trophies. One sometimes feels a little frightened when her beautiful varnished mahogany hull goes into action and she takes her place on a starting line filled with much clumsier-looking boats, her crew asserting their right to priority. Her displacement is not only smaller than that of her fellows but also smaller than that of boats of her age and size, so she accelerates infinitely faster and sails better close to the wind. Fortunately, the mop of white hair responsible for positioning her bow almost to the millimeter is a man who knows this boat through and through. He is Flavio Scala, a star helmsman formerly known as the eternal *timoniere* of *Azurra*, the twelve-meter class boat which the Italians entered for the America's Cup in 1983, when it was still being contested at Newport.

Apart from the fact that she was built more recently, *Agneta* takes us outside that handful of famous architects who worked in Britain or the United States at the beginning of the twentieth century. Her creator, the Swedish architect Knud Reimers, was at the same time her first owner, and christened her with the name of his daughter. Knowing this, we can better understand the reasons for her very streamlined form and her external appearance with a hull of varnished wood. The Swedes are very keen on these types of long, narrow, light boats, possibly prone to heeling but excellent when sailing close-hauled and able to accelerate smartly with the slightest breeze. As for the woodwork, this is the most prevalent raw material in a country where the major part of the land is covered by forest. *Agneta* was built at Stockholm in 1948 but changed owners in 1951, enjoying twenty years of good and loyal service with Sr. Agnelli. One of the most powerful men in Italy, and Europe too, he has always had a passion for the sea and has always had boats that were out of the ordinary — some of them very simple, like *Agneta*, others more extravagant like his enormous *Extrabeat*. His present boat, *Stealth*, has the same proportions — though in a bigger version — as an America's Cup class, and is unusual in being totally black from the base of the keel to the top of the mast, including the sails and carbon-fiber

deck gear. She is also regularly accompanied by a fast tender and an old tug painted the same color!

After the Agnelli era, *Agneta* moved to Sardinian waters — Porto Rotondo, to be precise — in 1981, when she was bought by Count Dona Delle Rose. Some time later she became the property of the Italian architect Giuseppe Andolina. It was then time for her to sail back up the Adriatic to Rimini and the yard of Carlini, to undergo a long refit which took no less than 18,000 hours' work. This operation was, of course, carried out with extreme care and attention, its target being to modify the boat's layout and the finish of the interior arrangements as well as her interior decoration. Nothing was left to chance at this jewel of a yard; some of the modifications were visualized and tested in advance on models, and the hearth of the main cabin had to be remade three times!

FAR LEFT
*With her long, narrow hull, Agneta is a miracle of decoration, using all the refinements possible given the wonderful properties of wood: detail of the bulwark bearing the boat's name; some folds of sailcloth; the saloon on the starboard side; a period lamp in a cabin.*

BELOW LEFT
*A general view of the cabin in the forward half of the boat. The pillar in the center is the mast.*

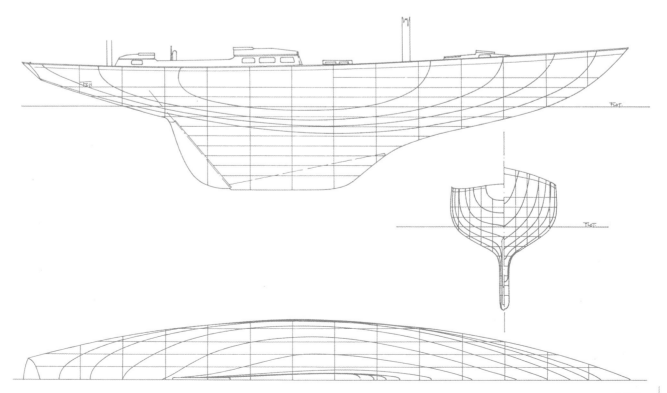

PAGES 184-5
Agneta *could almost
be the reincarnation of
an oceanic bird.*

RIGHT AND OPPOSITE
*Lines, shapes,
materials, colors
— with Agneta,
classic sails are
transformed into an
exercise in style.*

The interior arrangements on board *Agneta* are a real symphony of variations in the use of woodwork. Stained-glass set in marquetry conceals the boat's book collections, silk covers turn the seats into decorative objects, and the whole thing is a unique extravaganza, harmonizing the colors and textures of teak, pear wood, mahogany, and spruce. Numerous decorative objects have the good taste to date from the 1950s (including the radiotelephone set) and add a domestic note of exquisite delicacy, making *Agneta* a really exceptional boat. Since Giuseppe Andolina's death, his widow Raffaela Stefani has become passionately involved in continuing his work. Keeping the boat going, maintaining her in remarkable condition, and letting her be sailed by experienced hands, she ensures that the spirit which guided her husband is perpetuated. Boats are often full-blooded love stories, but if some can be seen as masculine, *Agneta* is most certainly feminine.

# The Nioulargue

The Nioulargue is no more than a tall story, a practical joke, a good time. The Nioulargue is never too serious, and that is the reason it has become so famous.

I t all started in 1981 with a drunken bet — at least it was during a meal, though a pretty liquid one, in the course of which a challenge was issued involving the American crew of Dick Jason's Swan *Pride* and that of the twelve-meter class *Ikra*, then skippered by Jean Laurrain. The course was a very simple one: starting at the foot of the Portalet tower, in front of the village of Saint-Tropez, and finishing at the Club 55 Restaurant on Pampelonne beach. The only race marker was the shallows of the Nioulargo, which is in fact a Provençal term meaning "sea nest."

It so happens that Patrice de Colmont, the owner of the restaurant, is not entirely like other men. He was born next to this lovely beach, lives there, and very seldom leaves it — his favorite village no less. Why should he? The whole world comes to him anyway, throughout the year. On the other hand, Patrice de Colmont and some of his friends have succeeded in perpetuating this challenge to the point where it has become a tremendous event, captivating all the crews, boat owners, and the entire world of sailing with its authentic yet relaxed spirit.

## The perfect niche

The Nioulargue takes place during the first week in October. In some fifteen years it has become a unique rally, allowing ordinary racing boats to compete at the same time as prestigious grand yachts, ultramodern prototypes, vintage yachts, and traditional local boats. There you meet anonymous crews, owners of every caliber, famous skippers, French people and foreigners — a lot of foreigners — and when the schedule allows, there are even challengers preparing for the America's Cup. Not bad for a drunken bet!

The essence of yachting is an indefinable mixture consisting of a love of the sea and of boats, a nonchalance stamped with certain feelings of aristocracy, and a pronounced taste for partying on land and for sailing skillfully on the open sea. In Saint-Tropez it has found a niche that measures up to its great traditions. It has also been no small achievement on the part of Patrice de Colmont, and of the active members of the Pampelonne Yacht Club, that over the years they have managed to retain the spirit of the original challenge between the crews of *Pride* and *Ikra*.

*ABOVE*
*Between the lateen-rigged boats and the half-closed shutters of the International Yacht Club of Pampelonne, the Nioulargue has grown because it has never taken itself too seriously.*

*OPPOSITE*
*Racing boats large and small, vintage yachts or modern racers — at the beginning of October, the Nioulargue brings every type of sailing boat together.*

I.Y.C.P

This was particularly true when, contrary to what was going on at nearby events, the Nioulargue was one of the first sailing regattas to refuse boats using their names as advertising. Similarly, they do not run after TV shows or PR companies, feeling it is important not to allow "business" to disturb or ensnare the participants. Even the race sponsors are merely "friends" who are obliged to go about things as discreetly as possible. And if by chance the crews should raid the posh guests of a "pirate ship," who have sailed no further than the cinema and now are holding a rather too private party on board, the organizers will heartily applaud the disrespectful creativity of the real sailors.

*THIS PAGE*
*Whether in the village itself, on the water or late in the evening, once a year Saint-Tropez lives to the rhythm of the Nioulargue.*

*OPPOSITE*
*The Nioulargue in all its splendor. The most famous of Provençal harbors is filled to bursting with the most beautiful boats in the world — a sight well worth a detour.*

### An unbeatable rendezvous

You get the point: the Nioulargue has become a really magnificent event, and one that it is quite impossible to miss if you have the good fortune to own a classic yacht or be a crew member on one. It is quite permissible to seek out a decrepit yacht at the end of some creek with the idea of refusing to allow it to die until it has revealed its history and demonstrated its beauty at the Nioulargue. Year after year, the event has seen the arrival of increasingly sumptuous classic yachts, their

numbers growing and turning the little harbor into the most tremendous concentration imaginable of beautiful hulls, sparkling varnish, elegant rigs, and vintage sails.

The Nioulargue, which fills its participants with pleasure, is also an event which allows the public to join the party. You need only take a short walk beside the sea and settle in the shade of a pine tree on the hillside below the citadel. From this impregnable promontory, you can watch the most beautiful yachts in the world sailing beneath your feet, while chewing on a sprig of rosemary or thyme. Nothing would then prevent you, except perhaps a phobia for crowds, from going for a drink at the Hôtel Sube overlooking the harbor, or, one floor down, from ordering a *pastis au mètre* at the Café de Paris.

*ABOVE*
*Parading lazily
beneath a gentle
autumn sun off the
Baie des Canebiers.*

*BELOW*
*Period costume and a
floating jazz band —
at the Nioulargue,
boats come in all
colors.*

*OPPOSITE*
*Who's who in this
crowded line-up at the
start of a race?*

*PAGES 196–7*
*At apéritif time, the
most beautiful yachts
in the world have at
last earned a rest. For
the crews, the night is
only just beginning …*

## The siren of the world's most beautiful boats

Like every living being, the Nioulargue has had its ups and its downs — the latter following a fatal accident. In 1996 there was a collision between the big schooner *Mariette* and the small six-meter class *Taos Brett IV*. The trial which followed caused the event to be suspended for three years, but there have been so many exceptional moments in previous rallies that this interruption is an apt opportunity to bring them all together. Those quite magical moments when everything is perfect: the autumn light, the wind, sometimes calm, sometimes violent, the boats, some of them more magnificent than others. A J-class sails by, scraping the breakwater and making its spectators tremble with emotion, a perfectly set gaff-rigger, the big yachts going about as they do in match racing near the starting line. At that hour when the sun begins to chisel the Massif des Maures into a series of bluish lines, our spirits are calmed by the sight of a Mediterranean craft going by with its lateen sails, the crew beaming and holding glasses of rosé in their hands. We can admire the maneuvers of *Pen Duick*, reaching its moorings in the mouse hole reserved for it in just a few impeccable moves; we can smile at the dozens of pairs of deck shoes massed together at the end of the gangway at apéritif time. And when, on a gray autumn morning, the sirens of the most beautiful yachts in the world sound to greet the first yacht to leave its moorings and set off for its winter berth, we are suddenly aware that the classic yacht season is well and truly finished, that summer has fled, that the party is over. The approaching winter suddenly feels very long …

# Glossary

**Arrangements** see **Interior arrangements**.

**Awning:** Protective cloth or material which can be stretched across the cockpit or deck area to protect the crew from the sun or in bad weather.

**Bermuda rig:** Rig characterized by the triangular shape of the mainsail.

**Bisquine:** French term for traditional lug rig with two or three masts and quadrilateral sails.

**Boom:** Horizontal spar supporting the mainsail and fixed aft of the mast and just above the deck. The boom makes it possible to secure the foot of the mainsail and support it when it is lowered.

**Boomkin:** The equivalent of a bowsprit, but located at the stern of a boat. It is used to support the stay supporting a mast further aft.

**Bowsprit:** Spar projecting from the stem, supporting the mast and allowing the sails to be set further forward and thus increase the boat's sail area.

**Broker:** Agent or intermediary who may manage, sell, buy, even supervise the construction or works on a boat on behalf of the owner.

**Bulkhead:** Transverse or longitudinal partition separating portions of a vessel. Some bulkheads are panels fitted to the interior of the boat to conceal the fabric of the hull or the structure of certain technical elements to give a more elegant appearance to the arrangements.

**Careen:** To put the hull of a boat on its side, or more particularly to lift the lower part out of the water.

**Chainplate:** Solid fittings to which the shrouds and stays are secured on the outer side of the hull.

**Choppy sea:** Irregular, broken water found close to land or when the wind has changed direction.

**Clipper:** Large trading ship from the mid-nineteenth century, embodying the apogee of the age of sail. Equipped with three, four or five masts and measuring more than 100 meters (330 feet) in length, clippers set many long-distance sailing records.

**Close-hauled:** Sailing as close into the wind as possible. It is impossible to sail directly into the wind, so sailors tack at an angle to the wind.

**Coach:** Usually a forward deck cabin, or part of the interior arrangements which protrudes upward through the line of the deck.

**Coil:** You coil a line by bending it in a circular shape. It can then be kept coiled by means of a knot.

**Collapse:** To collapse a sail is to bring it down from the rigging and flatten it. This operation is done when sailing is finished or when it is thought necessary to reduce the sail area.

**Coquiller:** Type of French fishing boat specializing in catching *coquille Saint-Jacques*.

**Cutter:** Boat rigged with a single mast and having two triangular sails before the mast: a jib (topsail) located high on the mast; and a staysail fixed at deck level. Modern boats generally carry a larger single foresail called a Genoa jib.

**Dead work:** Work that is carried out above the waterline and therefore is immediately visible.

**Deck gear:** General term for the mechanical equipment used on deck for maneuvers (blocks, winches, cleats, shackles etc.).

**Defender:** In the America's Cup there are only two competitors: the defender, which sails in the colors of the club holding the trophy; and the challenger, which tries to win it from the other.

**Displacement:** Universal term for the weight of a boat. According to Archimedes' Principle, it corresponds to the amount of water displaced when a boat is placed in the water or removed from it.

**Doghouse:** Outside cabin located on deck where the crew can shelter in rough weather.

**Ease, ease out:** Action of taking the tension off a rope, wire or cable. You can ease out a sheet or a mooring line.

**Fin keel:** In this type of keel, all the lead is located in a bulb beneath the keel to which are fixed lateral fins to improve its hydrodynamic qualities. The "anti-drift" function provided by this fin also makes the boat quick on the helm and therefore easy to steer. See also **Keel**.

**Freeboard:** The height of the hull above the waterline, usually measured amidships

**Gaff rig:** Rig characterized by a large trapezoidal fore and aft sail. A wooden spar extends the head of the sail.

**Guard rails:** Cables or wires stretched around the outer edge of the deck to protect the crew from falling overboard. They are supported at regular intervals on stanchions.

**Halyard:** Cable, wire or line for raising a sail, hoisting it to the top of the rigging. The halyard is later released to lower the sail.

**Haul:** Opposite of ease. Actions aimed at increasing the tension on a line or cable. You can haul on a halyard or a mooring line either by hand or with the help of a hoist or winch.

**Inshore/offshore:** Terms used to indicate whether a stretch of water is sheltered or not. An inshore regatta is contested close to land, in a harbor or bay. An offshore regatta is contested on the open sea.

**Interior arrangements:** Everything to do with the internal space of a boat (cabins, saloon, galley, heads, area for stowing sails etc.).

**Jib:** Triangular sail set forward of the mast and fixed to the forestay on the bowsprit or the stem.

**Jib-headed topsail:** In a gaff-rigged vessel, this is the triangular sail set above the mainsail. A gaff-rigged ketch sometimes has a topsail on the mainmast and the mizzen.

**Keel:** Shaped fin, often made of cast iron or lead, located under the boat and thanks to its weight serving as a counterbalance to the force of the wind in the sails, which tends to make the boat heel. The keel's surface also prevents the boat from drifting laterally when sailing against the wind. There is a distinction between the long keels, harmoniously married to the hull of the boat (the rule on all classic yachts), and the modern fins, which are smaller, deeper and more effective, but which also cause the boat to move less predictably.

**Kevlar:** Synthetic fiber developed by the Dupont de Nemours company. Extremely resistant, it is used to make modern hulls, some sailcloths, and lines with minimal stretch.

**Lateen sail:** Sail typically used on Mediterranean boats. A short mast supports a long spar on which a triangular sail is set.

**Lighter:** Type of cargo boat generally used for harbor work.

**Live work:** Work carried out below the waterline.

**Long keel** see **Keel**.

**Luff:** A boat (or its helmsman) luffs when she comes close to the wind. You luff to pass from a following wind to a crosswind, or to pass from a crosswind to sail close-hauled (into the wind). A luff is also the leading edge of a fore-and-aft sail.

**Mizzen:** The shorter mast aft of the mainmast on a ketch or yawl. Also, the third mast on a schooner with three or four masts.

**Mylar:** Transparent plastic film used to make sails. Applied as an outer coating, it fixes the sail material and stiffens it.

**Ocean-going cruiser:** Cruising boat intended for long-distance voyages, as opposed to coastal cruisers, which are generally smaller.

**Offshore** see **Inshore/offshore**.

**Pilot boat:** This type of swift, seaworthy boat was originally used by a pilot responsible for guiding ships into harbor. The pilot, a qualified coastal navigator with specific local knowledge, would board the ship from the pilot boat and be picked up by it when his job was done.

**Planking:** This forms the hull of the boat — the skin which makes it float, as opposed to the internal structures (frames and ribs) which serve as its skeleton. The planking can be of wood, metal or plastic. If the hull is made of several layers, these are referred to as internal or external planking.

**Pram:** Small rectangular-shaped boat or dinghy, sometimes attached to a larger boat and used for harbor transport etc.

**Reach:** Sailing with the wind pushing the boat from the general direction of the beam.

**Reefs:** When the wind is blowing, you need to reduce the surface of a sail. In its lower part there are strips of extra canvas called reef-bands to which reef-points (short lengths of small rope) are fixed, and these are then tied to shorten the sail.

**Rigging:** Broadly refers to everything which serves to support, raise and adjust the sails above the deck. In its narrower meaning, refers to the cables which hold up the mast. In present-day usage, the rigging of a boat means the geometry of its sail plan.

**Running rigging:** All the non-fixed lines, wires and cables which are used to maneuver the boat.

**Schooner:** Fore-and-aft-rigged sailing vessel with two or more masts. The forward mast must be shorter or of the same height as the others.

**Sheet:** Line fixed to the sail or the boom so that its position to the wind can be adjusted.

**Shroud:** Wire or cable supporting a mast to the sides of a vessel. Abreast of the mast, the shrouds are fixed to chainplates.

**Sloop:** Boat equipped with a single mast. It may be rigged as a cutter, with two foresails: a yankee and a staysail.

**Spar:** Wooden, metal or (in some modern boats) carbon-fiber pole which makes up the skeleton of the rigging.

Masts, booms, yards and gaffs are all of them spars.

**Spinnaker:** Large balloon sail used when the wind is aft of the beam.

**Spinnaker boom:** Special boom used to raise a spinnaker and consisting of a long spar of wood or metal tubing, which can be fixed to the foredeck and used horizontally to push the sail into position.

**Spreaders:** Horizontal struts fitted to the side of the mast and serving to spread shrouds and stays outward.

**Stay:** Wire or cable supporting a mast fore or aft.

**Staysail:** Fore-and-aft sail which is set up on a stay.

**Steering wheel:** Helm with a circular or wheel shape, as opposed to the straight tiller found on smaller boats.

**Tender:** Small boat attached to a larger vessel, used in repair work or to transport guests and supplies.

**Tiller:** Straight helm found on smaller boats.

**Vectran:** Composite fiber, extremely supple and very resistant to stretching, used to make certain lines or sails.

**Winch:** Piece of deck equipment used for hauling on a line, wire or cable. Some winches are reserved for specific maneuvers, e.g. the halyard winch is used only for adjusting the halyards.

**Yawl rig:** Boat with two masts, with a shorter mast aft stepped abaft the rudder-stock.

# Acknowledgments

A book such as this could not have been produced without the help of owners, skippers, crews, organizers, writers, journalists, researchers, photographers and publishers, both past and present, who by their work, passion, knowledge and know-how have added a stone to the edifice of the world of classic yachts.

Thanks are due to:
Daniel Allisy, Hervé Hillard, Didier Ravon and the Voiles et Voiliers team, the Associazione Italiana Vele Epoca (AIVE), John Bardon, Jerôme Boyer, Daniel Charles, William Collier, Bernard d'Alessandri and the team from the Monaco Yacht club, François-Jean Daehn, Patrice de Colmont and the team from the Pampelonne Yacht Club, Emmanuel de Toma, Bernard Deguy, Noëlle Duck, Robert H. Edy, Christian Février and Annie Fyot, Martin Francis, Jean Guilhem, Serge and Anne-Marie Guillaumou, Klaus Hebben, Malcolm J. Horsley, Mr. and Mrs. Ernst Klaus, Luigi Lang, Pierre and Dominique Lembo, Philippe Lechevallier, Jacques Louvet, Ian McAllisters, Jean-Pierre Odero and the team from the Cannes Yacht Club, Philip and Marie Plisson, Guillaume Plisson, Hubert Poilroux, Erwan Quéméré, Guy Ribadeau-Dumas, Rachel Rising and the team from Strategic Advertising, Julien Rondeau, Gérard Simonetti-Malaspina, Mme. Rafaela Stefani, Éric Tabarly (deceased), Mme. Jacqueline Tabarly, Jacques Taglang, Patrick Teboul, Bruno Troublé and the team from Jour J, Maguelonne Turcat, Gérard Vachet, the firm of Louis Vuitton Malletier, the Yacht Club Costa Smeralda.

Special thanks to:
Michel Buntz, Lina Chocteau and the team from the Arlequin/Picto laboratory — Marseille, Xavier Chaubert, Philippe Holder, Daniel Manoury and Dominique Romet, helicopter pilots, and all the staff at Pêcheur d'Images.

PHOTOGRAPHIC CREDITS
The photographs in this book are all © Gilles Martin-Raget and may be ordered from him (tel. +33 (0)4 91 31 44 71/fax +33 (0)4 91 31 57 40/e-mail: gmr@martin-raget.com/website: http://martin-raget.com), with the following exceptions:
© Erwan Quéméré, page 141 (bottom);
© Kos, pages 132 (two interior photos), 173 (two interior photos, below right);
© Carlo Borlenghi, pages 65 (below right), 68, 141 (three top photos).
We thank them for their willing collaboration.

First published in the United States of America in 2000 by
Abbeville Publishing Group
22 Cortlandt Street
New York, NY 10007

First published in 1998 by Editions du Chêne-Hachette Livre
Original title: Yachts classiques
Written and illustrated by: Gilles Martin-Raget
Drawings by: François Chevalier

© 1998 Editions du Chêne-Hachette Livre, Paris, France
© 2000 English language edition, Abbeville Publishing Group, New York, USA

English-language edition prepared by:
Translate-A-Book, Oxford, England
Translator: Michael Leitch
American Editors: Bob McKenna, Richard Koss
General Editor: Andrew Shackleton
Typesetting: Organ Graphic, Abingdon, England
Printed by: Canale, Italy
Bound by: AGM, France

First edition
2 4 6 8 10 9 7 5 3 1

Library of Congress Cataloging-in-Publication Data

Martin-Raget, Gilles.
    Legendary yachts / Gilles Martin-Raget.
        p. cm.
    ISBN 0-7892-0637-4
    I. Yachts. I. Title.

VM331 .M375 2000
386'.2223—dc21

99-088024